SELECTED WRITINGS

BENJAMIN FRANKLIN

SELECTED WRITINGS

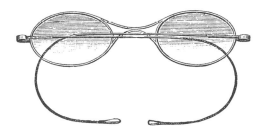

FALL RIVER PRESS

Cover art © North Wind Picture Archives/Alamy (printing press);
© The Print Collector/Heritage/The Image Works (handwriting);
© iStockphoto (paper background); © Corbis (diagram of
Franklin's electrical apparatus)

Cover art direction by Jo Obarowski
Book design by HSU + ASSOCIATES

Fall River Press
122 Fifth Avenue
New York, NY 10011

ISBN: 978-1-4351-1989-5

Printed and bound in China

1 3 5 7 9 10 8 6 4 2

CONTENTS

Political Writings and Satires

Letters

The Maxims of Poor Richard

FOREWORD

Writer. Statesman. World-traveler. Publisher. Inventor. Philosopher. Printer. Diplomat. Newspaper editor. Scientist. Satirist. Pamphleteer. Social critic. Of all America's illustrious Founding Fathers, Benjamin Franklin was the one who most readily wore the mantle of the Renaissance Man. His interests were remarkably eclectic, and his talents extraordinarily diverse. A signer of the Declaration of Independence, a founder of the subscription library system, inventor of bifocal eyeglasses and the lightning rod, and an originator of the city of Philadelphia's first fire department, Franklin might have gone on to a distinguished career in any of the disciplines for which he showed enthusiasm. Today, we remember him as a writer of some of the wittiest and most stimulating essays and articles published during our nation's Colonial era, all informed by his boundless intellectual curiosity and openminded spirit of inquiry.

Franklin was born in Boston, Massachusetts on January 17, 1706, the youngest of ten sons (and the fifteenth of seventeen children) born to a soap and candle maker who had fled to the New World to escape religious persecution. He entered grammar school at the age of eight, and after one year was transferred to a school for writing and arithmetic. His formal education ended at age ten when he was taken from school to assist his father in the family business. After two years working at this trade, for which he had little fondness, Franklin was apprenticed to his brother James, who published the *New England Courant.*

At the time, it was customary that those who printed newspapers wrote most or all of their content. As part of his program to master writing skills,

Franklin began submitting contributions to the paper anonymously, slipping them under the door at night and listening to the comments James and his friends offered at the office the next day. He began writing for the *Courant* in 1722, when he was just sixteen years old. Between April 2 to October 8, he contributed fourteen essays bylined "Silence Dogood," who presented herself as a young widow with strong opinions on issues ranging from social customs to religion and government. In his *Autobiography*, Franklin reports having come upon a volume of Joseph Addison and Richard Steele's *The Spectator*, which was appearing at that time in England, and being "much delighted with it." The Dogood essays were the culmination of Franklin's effort to write in emulation of *The Spectator*, and its objective "to enliven morality with wit, and to temper wit with morality." Light and satirical, these essays are the first examples of an approach Franklin would take in much of his writing, creating a fictional persona as the mouthpiece for opinions that range from the commonsense and practical to the outrageous. In much of his writing thereafter, Franklin cultivated and developed alter egos whose opinions presented one perspective—sometimes ill-informed, sometimes simply that of an ordinary person—on an issue and challenged the reader to debate it with his or her own.

For a brief time in 1722 Franklin acted as the *Courant's* manager while his brother served a short prison sentence for criticizing the local authorities. Upon his discharge James was enjoined to no longer print the newspaper. He tried to circumvent this by naming Benjamin the publisher, and though the ruse worked with authorities the complications it created with regard to Benjamin's indenture to James led to a rift between the brothers. Franklin fled to Philadelphia, and then in 1724 sailed to England where he learned typesetting. He returned to Philadelphia in 1726 and took up work with

William Keimer, whom he had worked for as a journeyman before his travels abroad. Soon thereafter the two men had a falling out, and when Keimer founded the *Universal Instructor in All Arts and Sciences: and Pennsylvania Gazette*, partly to forestall his employee's ambition to start up his own newspaper, Franklin took his services to Keimer's competitor, the *American Weekly Mercury*. With the help of members of the Junto, a literary salon that he had formed, Franklin authored "The Busy-Body," a series of essays represented as the work of a nosy and censorious observer of his times. Like the Dogood essays, the Busy-Body pieces were lightly satiric essays that poked as much fun at the narrowminded opinions of their fictional narrator as at the foibles of those people whom he criticized. Keimer believed that at least one of the essays was directed at him and threatened lawsuit. Ultimately, Franklin had the last laugh: Keimer's paper faltered financially, and Franklin bought it and abbreviated its name as the *Pennsylvania Gazette*. It was to become a major outlet for his writing until the 1750s.

The thirty-one years Franklin spent in Philadelphia are generally acknowledged as the years he achieved his maturity as a writer. The variety of styles he attempted and the breadth of subjects he tackled are remarkable, especially considering the frequency with which he produced his articles, essays, and pamphlets. He continued in the vein of the Silence Dogood articles, writing self-satirizing letters to the editor of the *Gazette* authored by pseudonymous correspondents such as "Anthony Afterwit," "Celia Single," and "Alice Addertongue." These brief missives, with their observations on the battle of the sexes, the hazards of social climbing, and the fine art of character assassination are unique comic monologues that turn the character flaws of their all-too-human narrators into foundations for light moral lectures. In hindsight, we recognize these pieces as training for the approach Franklin would take in *Poor Richard's Almanack*, the pseudonymous compendium of agricultural insights, astronomical study, and folk wisdom that he published in annual installments from 1733 to 1758. Known today largely for the aphorisms and folk-wisdom it collected in each installment, the almanack was Franklin's bestselling work in his lifetime Richard Saunders, the imaginary author of the almanack, is a unique figure in American literature, a bumbling amateur astrologer whose predictions never came true but who won the sympathies of his readers through the genial and good-natured persona Franklin crafted for him.

The indirect approach of these humorous articles, whose authors showed how indefensible their absurd viewpoints were by defending them so strongly, is the same tack Franklin took in several Swiftian essays that pursued the illogic of their arguments to logical extremes. "A Witch Trial at Mount Holly" evokes the scientific method in its suggestion that the ridiculous and sometimes lethal tests by which accused witches were condemned should be inflicted on their righteous persecutors who should have no fear of them. "Rattle-Snakes as Felons" chastises England for its policy of transporting convicted felons to the colonies through its suggestion that sending poisonous rattlesnakes from America to the mother country would be a form of reciprocal exchange. "The Art of Saying Little in Much" makes it case for directness and brevity in communications by reproducing the self-serving petition of an Irish lawyer that is full of bombastic hyperbole and run-on sentences.

"The Art of Saying Little in Much" can be read as a bookend to the more serious essay "On Simplicity," in which Franklin reflects that "Simplicity is the homespun Dress of Honesty, and Chicanery and Craft are the Tinsel Habits and the false Elegance which are worn to cover the Deformity of Vice and Knavery." Some of Franklin's best writing takes the form of brief meditations and sober sermons in which humor is kept to a minimum. Essays such as "On Constancy," which finds a want of "Steadiness and Perseverance" in pursuit of goals to be an obstacle to personal achievement, and "Advice to a Young Tradesman Written by an Old One," which emphasizes "Industry and Frugality" in all business matters, are masterpieces of rhetoric that state their cases succinctly and argue their points logically. Franklin's best-known work in this vein is "The Way to Wealth," which uses maxims from twenty years of installments of the lighthearted *Poor Richard's Almanack* as the foundation for a sober essay on the exercise of industry, frugality, and prudence in the achievement of financial success. Published in 1774, this pamphlet was still in print a century later and is one of the most reprinted works in American literature.

Though he wrote on a wide variety of topics, certain themes regularly engaged Franklin's attention. Drunkenness as an illustration of failed character was the inspiration for several serious essays, but also for the delightful "Drinkers Dictionary," a compilation of more than 200 slang terms for being drunk that, by their profusion, hint at just how well-known and widespread such overindulging was. By the 1750s, the theme that dominates Franklin's essays is the deteriorating relationship between the colonies and England. As a patriot to his native land, Franklin was passionate in his defense of the colonies against what he (and others) saw as the increasing irrationality and injustice of the remote monarchy that governed them. Employing the rhetorical skills he had honed over more than thirty years of writing, Franklin penned numerous essays that rank with the work of Thomas Paine,

Thomas Jefferson, Alexander Hamilton, and others as the most important writing published during America's Revolutionary War period. "Humorous Reasons for Restoring Canada" is written tongue-in-cheek from the viewpoint of a British citizen who offers eleven reasons why giving Canada back to France is best for the British Empire. For example: "We should restore Canada, that we may soon have a new war, and another opportunity of spending two or three millions a year in Americs; there being great danger of our growing too rich, our European expences not being sufficient to drain our immense treasures." "An Edict by the King of Prussia" draws amusing parallels between the colonies and England in its recommendation that Prussia (to which England was tied through its royal bloodline) begin imposing on England that same commercial regulations that England was imposing on the American colonies. "Rules by Which a Great Empire May be Reduced to a Small One" is a rhetorical masterpiece in which Franklin assumes that the alienation and disaffection that British rule is engendering in the colonies is an actual objective of the Crown, and offers twenty soundly argued points on how continuing the worse abuses of the monarchy will ensure the achievement of that objective.

From 1757 until his death in 1790, Franklin spent very little time in America. Political missions on behalf of the Pennsylvania, and later New Jersey, Massachusetts, and Georgia Assemblies drew him to England up through 1775. Some of his most revolutionary writing appeared during these years and first saw print in publications of his friends in England. From 1776 to 1785, he served as an American ambassador to France where his efforts were crucial for drumming up foreign support for the colonies' revolt against England. Franklin lived long enough not only to put his signature on his nation's Declaration of Independence but also to advocate with great eloquence, in his "Speech in the Constitutional Convention at the Conclusion of Its Deliberations," the adoption and ratification of the United States Constitution.

More than two centuries after his death, Benjamin Franklin is remembered as the author of *Poor Richard's Almanack*, a milestone in America's early literary history, and his *Autobiography*, which was not published in its full form until the late nineteenth century but has since achieved the status of a landmark of American letters. The divisions created for presenting his writings in this book are somewhat artificial as they were imposed in hindsight on his vast and varied body of work. Franklin wrote serious essays at the same time that he wrote amusing *jeux d'esprit*, and some of his most sober essays and reflections are laced with the subversive wit and humor that were his trademarks. His letters, essays, and articles are all distinguished by concision, and an exemplary economy of style. These works, and the qualities that make them so memorable, are among his most enduring contributions to American letters.

EPITAPH

The Body of
B. Franklin,
Printer;
Like the Cover of an old Book,
Its Contents torn out,
And stript of its Lettering and Gilding,
Lies here, Food for Worms.
But the Work shall not be wholly lost:
For it will, as he believ'd, appear once more,
In a new & more perfect Edition,
Corrected and amended
By the Author.
He was born Jan. 6th, 1706.
Died   17

1728

ESSAYS
AND
DIVERSIONS

PRINTER'S ERRORS

To the Publisher of the Pennsylvania Gazette.

Printerum est errare.

SIR,

As your last Paper was reading in some Company where I was present, these Words were taken Notice of in the Article concerning Governor *Belcher*, [*After which his Excellency, with the Gentlemen trading to New-England*, died *elegantly at Pontack's*.] The Word *died* should doubtless have been *dined, Pontack's* being a noted Tavern and Eating-house in *London* for Gentlemen of Condition; but this Omission of the letter (*n*) in that Word, gave us as much Entertainment as any Part of your Paper. One took the Opportunity of telling us, that in a certain Edition of the Bible, the Printer had, where *David* says *I am fearfully and wonderfully made*, omitted the Letter (*e*) in the last Word, so that it was, *I am fearfully and wonderfully mad*; which occasion'd an ignorant Preacher, who took that Text, to harangue his Audience for half an hour on the Subject of *Spiritual Madness*. Another related to us, that when the Company of Stationers in *England* had the Printing of the Bible in their Hands, the Word (*not*) was left out in the Seventh Commandment, and the whole Edition was printed off with *Thou shalt commit Adultery*, instead of *Thou shalt not*, &c. This material *Erratum* induc'd the Crown to take the Patent from them which is now held by the King's Printer. The *Spectator's* Remark upon this Story is, that he doubts many of our modern Gentlemen have this faulty Edition by 'em, and are not made sensible of the Mistake. A Third Person in the Company acquainted us with an unlucky Fault that went through a whole Impression of Common-Prayer-Books; in the Funeral Service, where these Words are, *We shall all be changed in a moment, in the twinkling of an Eye*, &c. the Printer had omitted the (*c*) in *changed*, and it read thus, *We shall all be hanged*, &c. And lastly, a Mistake of your Brother News-Printer was mentioned, in *The Speech of* James Prouse *written the Night before he was to have been executed*, instead of *I die a Protestant*, he has put it, *I died a Protestant*. Upon the whole you came off with the more favourable Censure, because your Paper is most commonly very correct, and yet you were never known to triumph upon it, by publickly ridiculing and exposing the continual Blunders of your Contemporary. Which Observation was concluded by a good old Gentleman in Company, with this general just Remark, That whoever accustoms himself to pass over in Silence the Faults of his Neighbours, shall meet with much better Quarter from the World when he happens to fall into a Mistake himself; for the Satyrical and Censorious, whose Hand is against every Man, shall upon such Occasions have every Man's Hand against him.

I am, SIR, your Friend, &c.

J. T.

The Pennsylvania Gazette, MARCH 13, 1729/30

RULES AND MAXIMS
FOR PROMOTING
MATRIMONIAL HAPPINESS

Ver novum, ver jam canorum, vere natus Orbis est:
Vere concordant amores, vere nubent alites—CATUL.

Fælices ter, & amplius,
   Quos irrupta tenet Copula: nec malis
Divulsis Querimoniis
    Suprema citius solvet amor die. —HORAT.

The happy State of Matrimony is, undoubtedly, the surest and most lasting Foundation of Comfort and Love; the Source of all that endearing Tenderness and Affection which arises from Relation and Affinity; the grand Point of Property; the Cause of all good Order in the World, and what alone preserves it from the utmost Confusion; and, to sum up all, the Appointment of infinite Wisdom for these great and good Purposes. Notwithstanding, such is the Perverseness of human Nature, and so easy is it to misuse the best of Things, that by the Folly and Ill-behaviour of those who enter into it, this is very often made a State of the most exquisite Wretchedness and Misery; which gives the wild and vicious Part of Mankind but too much reason to rail against it, and treat it with Contempt. Wherefore, it highly becomes the virtuous of both Sexes, by the Prudence of their Conduct, to redeem this noble Institution from those unjust

Reproaches which it at present labours under, and restore it to the Honour and Esteem it merits, by endeavouring to make each other as happy as they can.

I am now about to lay down such Rules and Maxims as I think most practicable and conducive towards the End and Happiness of Matrimony. And these I address to all Females that would be married, or are already so; not that I suppose their Sex more faulty than the other, and most to want Advice, for I assure them, upon my Honour, I believe the quite contrary; but the Reason is, because I esteem them better disposed to receive and practice it, and therefore am willing to begin, where I may promise myself the best Success. Besides, if there is any Truth in Proverbs, *Good Wives* usually make *Good Husbands.*

RULES and MAXIMS for promoting Matrimonial
Happiness. *Address'd to all* Widows, Wives, *and* Spinsters.

The likeliest Way, either to obtain a *good Husband*, or to keep one *so*, is to be *Good* yourself.

Never use a *Lover* ill whom you design to make your *Husband*, lest he either upbraid you with it, or return it afterwards: and if you find, at any Time, an Inclination to play the Tyrant, remember these two Lines of Truth and Justice.

Gently shall those be rul'd, *who gently sway'd;*
Abject *shall those* obey, *who* haughty *were* obey'd.

Avoid, both before and after Marriage, all Thoughts of *managing* your Husband. Never endeavour to deceive or impose on his Understanding: nor give him *Uneasiness* (as some do very foolishly) to *try* his Temper; but treat him always beforehand with *Sincerity*, and afterwards with *Affection* and *Respect*.

Be not over sanguine before Marriage, nor promise your self Felicity without Alloy, for that's impossible to be attain'd in this present State of Things. Consider beforehand, that the Person you are going to spend your Days with, is a Man, and not an Angel; and if, when you come together, you discover any Thing in his Humour or Behaviour that is not altogether so agreeable as you expected, *pass it over as a humane Frailty*: smooth your Brow; compose your Temper; and try to amend it by *Cheerfulness* and Good-nature.

Remember always, that whatever Misfortunes may happen to either, they are not to be charg'd to the Account of *Matrimony*, but to the Accidents and Infirmities of humane Life, a Burthen which each has engaged to assist the other in supporting, and to which both Parties are equally expos'd. Therefore, instead of *Murmurs*, *Reflections*, and *Disagreement*, whereby the *Weight* is rendred abundantly more *grievous*, readily put your Shoulders to the Yoke, and make it easier to both.

Resolve every Morning to be *good-natur'd* and CHEERFUL that Day: and if any Accident should happen to break that Resolution, suffer it not to put you out of Temper with every Thing besides, and especially with your Husband.

Dispute not with him, be the Occasion what it will; but much rather deny yourself the trivial Satisfaction of having your own Will, or gaining the better of an Argument, than risk a Quarrel or create an Heart-burning, which it's impossible to know the End of.

Be assured, a Woman's Power, as well as Happiness, has no other Foundation but her Husband's Esteem and Love, which consequently it is her undoubted Interest by all Means possible to preserve and increase. Do you, therefore, study his Temper, and command your own; enjoy his Satisfaction with him, share and sooth his Cares, and with the utmost Diligence conceal his Infirmities.

Read frequently with due Attention the Matrimonial Service; and take care in doing so, not to overlook the Word *Obey*.

In your Prayers be sure to add a Clause for Grace to make you a good Wife; and at the same Time, resolve to do your utmost endeavour towards it.

Always wear your Wedding Ring, for therein lies more Virtue than usually is imagined. If you are ruffled unawares, assaulted with improper Thoughts, or tempted in any kind against your Duty, cast your Eyes upon it, and call to Mind, who gave it you, where it was received, and what passed at that solemn Time.

Let the Tenderness of your conjugal Love be expressed with such Decency, Delicacy and Prudence, as that it may appear plainly and thorowly distinct from the designing Fondness of an Harlot.

Have you any Concern for your own Ease, or for your Husband's Esteem? then, have a due Regard to his Income and Circumstances in all your Expences and Desires: For if Necessity should follow, you run the greatest Hazard of being deprived of both.

Let not many Days pass together without a serious Examination how you have behaved as a Wife, and if upon Reflection you find your self guilty of any Foibles or Omissions, the best Attonement is, to be exactly careful of your future Conduct.

I am fully persuaded, that a strict Adherence to the foregoing Rules would equally advance the Honour of Matrimony, and the *Glory* of the *Fair Sex*: And since the greatest Part of them, with a very little Alteration, are as proper for Husbands as for Wives to practice, I recommend them accordingly to their Consideration, and hope, in a short time, to receive Acknowledgments from *married Persons* of *both Sexes* for the Benefit they receive thereby.

And now, in behalf of my *unlearned Readers*, I beg Leave of my *learned Ones*, to conclude this Discourse with Mr. *Creech*'s Translation of that Part of *Horace* which I have taken for the *Motto* of this Paper.

> *Thrice happy* They, *that free from* Strife,
> *Maintain a* Love *as long as Life:*
> *Whose fixt and binding Vows,*
> *No intervening* Jealousy,
> *No* Fears *and no* Debates *untye;*
> *And* Death *alone can loose.*

The Pennsylvania Gazette, OCTOBER 8, 1730

A WITCH TRIAL
AT MOUNT HOLLY

Burlington, Oct. 12. Saturday last at *Mount-Holly*, about 8 Miles from this Place, near 300 People were gathered together to see an Experiment or two tried on some Persons accused of Witchcraft. It seems the Accused had been charged with making their Neighbours Sheep dance in an uncommon Manner, and with causing Hogs to speak, and sing Psalms, &c. to the great Terror and Amazement of the King's good and peaceable Subjects in this Province; and the Accusers being very positive that if the Accused were weighed in Scales against a Bible, the Bible would prove too heavy for them; or that, if they were bound and put into the River, they would swim; the said Accused desirous to make their Innocence appear, voluntarily offered to undergo the said Trials, if 2 of the most violent of their Accusers would be tried with them. Accordingly the Time and Place was agreed on, and advertised about the Country; The Accusers were 1 Man and 1 Woman: and the Accused the same. The Parties being met, and the People got together, a grand Consultation was held, before they proceeded to Trial; in which it was agreed to use the Scales first; and a Committee of Men were appointed to search the Men, and a Committee of Women to search the Women, to see if they had any Thing of Weight about them, particularly Pins. After the Scrutiny was over, a huge great Bible belonging to the Justice of the Place was provided, and a Lane through the Populace was made from the Justices House to the Scales, which were fixed on a Gallows erected for that

Purpose opposite to the House, that the Justice's Wife and the rest of the Ladies might see the Trial without coming amongst the Mob; and after the Manner of *Moorfields*, a large Ring was also made. Then came out of the House a grave tall Man carrying the Holy Writ before the supposed Wizard, &c. (as solemnly as the Sword-bearer of *London* before the Lord Mayor) the Wizard was first put in the Scale, and over him was read a Chapter out of the Books of *Moses*, and then the Bible was put in the other Scale, (which being kept down before) was immediately let go; but to the great Surprize of the Spectators, Flesh and Bones came down plump, and outweighed that great good Book by abundance. After the same Manner, the others were served, and their Lumps of Mortality severally were too heavy for *Moses* and all the Prophets and Apostles. This being over, the Accusers and the rest of the Mob, not satisfied with this Experiment, would have the Trial by Water; accordingly a most solemn Procession was made to the Mill-pond, where both Accused and Accusers being stripp'd (saving only to the Women their Shifts) were bound Hand and Foot, and severally placed in the Water, lengthways, from the Side of a Barge or Flat, having for Security only a Rope about the Middle of each, which was held by some in the Flat. The Accuser Man being thin and spare, with some Difficulty began to sink at last; but the rest every one of them swam very light upon the Water. A Sailor in the Flat jump'd out upon the Back of the Man accused, thinking to drive him down to the Bottom; but the Person bound, without any Help, came up some time before the other. The Woman Accuser, being told that she did not sink, would be duck'd a second Time; when she swam again as light as before. Upon which she declared, That she believed the Accused had bewitched her to make her so light, and that she would be duck'd again a Hundred Times, but she would duck the Devil out of her. The accused Man, being surpriz'd at his own Swimming, was not so confident of his Innocence as before, but said, *If I am a Witch, it is more than I know.* The more thinking Part of the Spectators were of Opinion, that any Person so bound and plac'd in the Water (unless they were mere Skin and Bones) would swim till their Breath was gone, and their Lungs fill'd with Water. But it being the general Belief of the Populace, that the Womens Shifts, and the Garters with which they were bound help'd to support them; it is said they are to be tried again the next warm Weather, naked.

The Pennsylvania Gazette, OCTOBER 22, 1730

ON SIMPLICITY

There is in Humane Nature a certain charming Quality, innate and original to it, which is called SIMPLICITY. In latter Ages, this has been almost universally exploded, and banished from amongst Men, as the Characteristic of Folly; whilst *Cunning* and *Artifice* have prevailed in its stead, and with equal Justice been dignified with the Titles of Wisdom and Understanding. But I believe the juster Account of the Matter is, that Simplicity is the homespun Dress of Honesty, and Chicanery and Craft are the Tinsel Habits and the false Elegance which are worn to cover the Deformity of Vice and Knavery.

In the first Ages of the World, when Men had no Wants but what were purely natural, before they had refin'd upon their Necessities, and Luxury and Ambition had introduced a Thousand fantastick Forms of Happiness, Simplicity was the Dress and Language of the World, as Nature was its Law. The little Cunning which was then in use, only taught them to ensnare, or to make tame such Animals as were necessary to their Support or their Convenience, and were otherwise too swift or too strong for them; but since these Arts have attain'd their utmost Perfection, Men have practised the same low Stratagems upon one another, and by an infinite Variety of Disguises and well-covered Treacheries, have long since instituted those little Basenesses among the necessary Arts and Knowledges of Life, and practised without Scruple, that which they have long owned without Shame.

But if we look into the History of the World, and into the Characters of those who have had the greatest Names in it, we shall find, that this original Simplicity of Mind has gradually been worn off in every Age, down to the present Time, when there is hardly any Characters of it remaining undefaced. The old Greeks and Romans, whose unperishable Writings have preserved to us the Actions and Manners of their Countrymen, and who were so well studied in all the Forms and reasonable Happinesses of Life, are so full of that just and beautiful Stile and Sentiment, as seems to have been the only proper Method of transcribing the frank and open Characters of the Heroes they celebrate, and of making them and their Writers immortal.

To prove the natural Charm and Beauty there is in this Simplicity, we need only, at this Day, as false as the World is grown, retire but far enough from great Cities, the Scenes of all worldly Business and Action; and, I believe, the most cunning Man will be obliged to own, the high and sincere Pleasure there is in conversing from the Heart, and without Design. What Relief do we find in the simple and unaffected Dialogues of uncorrupted Peasants, after the tiresome Grimace of the Town! The veriest Double-Dealer in the World is ever hankering after an Opportunity to open his own Heart, tho' perhaps he curses himself after he has done it. We are all forward enough to protest and complain against the Falshood and Treachery of Mankind, tho' the Remedy be always in our own Power, and each is at Liberty to reform himself.

But perhaps we need not be forced always to go into the Country in search of this amiable Complexion of Mind, Simplicity; for I believe it will be found sometimes, that the Men of the truest Genius and highest Characters in the Conduct of the World, (as few of them as rise in any Age) are observed to possess this Quality in the highest Degree. They are Pretenders only, to Policy and Business, who have recourse to Cunning, and the little Chicaneries thereof: for Cunning is but the Ape of Wisdom, as Sheepishness is of Modesty, Impudence of Courage, and Pedantry of Learning.—Cunning, says my Lord *Bacon*, is a sinister or crooked Wisdom, and Dissimulation but a faint kind of Policy; for it asks a strong Wit and a strong Heart, to know when to tell Truth and to do it; therefore they are the weaker sort of Politicians, that are the greatest Dissemblers. And certainly there is a great Difference between a cunning Man and a wise One, not only in point of Honesty but in point of Ability; as there are those that can pack the Cards, who cannot play the Game well.

Cunning is a Vice purely personal, and is with the greatest Difficulty practised in free and mixed Assemblies. A cunning Man is obliged to hunt his Game alone, and to live in the dark; he is uncapable of Counsel and Advice, for his dishonest Purpose dies upon Discovery. A vertuous and an honourable Action only, will bear a Conference and Freedom of Debate. And this is the Part of true Wisdom, to be busy and assistant in a fair and worthy Design. None but Fools are Knaves, for wise Men cannot help being honest. Cunning therefore is the Wisdom of a Fool; one who has Designs that he dare not own.

To draw these loose Thoughts towards an End. If Cunning were any real Excellence in Human Nature, how comes it that the greatest and ablest, the most amiable and worthy of Mankind, are often entirely without it, and vastly above it; while Numbers of the weaker Part are observed to be very expert therein; sordid and ignorant Servants, and dishonest idle Vagabonds, often attain to the highest Perfection in it. Simplicity we are sure is natural, and the highest Beauty of Nature; and all that is excellent in Arts which Men have invented, is either to demonstrate this native Simplicity and Truth in Nature, or to teach us to transcribe and copy in every Thing from it. Simplicity of Speech and Manners is the highest Happiness as well as the greatest Ornament of Life; whereas nothing is so tiresome to one's self, as well as so odious to others, as Disguise and Affectation. Who was ever cunning enough to conceal his being so? No Mask ever hid it self. In a Word, those cunning Men, tho' they are not declared Enemies to the World, yet they are really Spies upon it, and ought in the Justice of Things to be considered and treated as such, whenever they are caught. And to what purpose is all this Craft? To make themselves suspected and avoided by the World in return, and to have never a Friend in it. A Knave cannot have a Friend, any more than he can be one: An honest Man must discover him, a Rascal will betray him. And by this Time I hope my Reader and I are agreed, that Wisdom and Vertue are the same Thing, as Knavery and Cunning are generally so too; and that for the future, we shall resolve to be what we would seem, which is the only sure way not to be afraid to seem what we really are.

Perhaps it is not necessary to add here, that by Simplicity is not at all meant the Pretences to it, which are made now a-days, by many good People, who I believe very honestly mistake the Thing, and while they aim at Simplicity are guilty of very gross Affectation. The Plainness and Integrity of Mind, which is here recommended, is very little concerned in any Quaintness of Habit, or Oddness of Behaviour: Nor is it at all of Importance to Vertue and Simplicity, that great care is taken to appear unfashionable. Again, on the other side, I know very well that the Word *Cunning* did in the ancient Sense of it imply Knowledge. The Word Ken may perhaps be akin to it; it is of Saxon Original, and we are told the Word King is derived from it. I have no Quarrel to this Construction of it; but only against (what it now comes to signify) the little Subtilty of base Minds, who are incapable of great and honest Actions; in which Sense the Word is now commonly used.

After all, I am sensible this crooked Wisdom has established itself by the Force of an unhappy Fashion, too firmly to be immediately exploded; and though I could wish my Reader would be ashamed to live in the World by such a wretched Method, yet I would warn him to be well aware of those that do; and to be sure to arm against them, not with the same Weapons, but those which are of much better Proof, the Integrity of a wise Man, and the Wisdom of an honest one.

The Pennsylvania Gazette, APRIL 13, 1732

ANTHONY AFTERWIT

Mr. Gazetteer,

I am an honest Tradesman, who never meant Harm to any Body. My Affairs went on smoothly while a Batchelor; but of late I have met with some Difficulties, of which I take the Freedom to give you an Account.

About the Time I first address'd my present Spouse, her Father gave out in Speeches, that if she married a Man he liked, he would give with her £200 on the Day of Marriage. 'Tis true he never said so to me, but he always receiv'd me very kindly at his House, and openly countenanc'd my Courtship. I form'd several fine Schemes, what to do with this same £200, and in some Measure neglected my Business on that Account: But unluckily it came to pass, that when the old Gentleman saw I was pretty well engag'd, and that the Match was too far gone to be easily broke off; he, without any Reason given, grew very angry, forbid me the House, and told his Daughter that if she married me he would not give her a Farthing. However (as he foresaw) we were not to be disappointed in that Manner; but having stole a Wedding, I took her home to my House, where we were not in quite so poor a Condition as the Couple describ'd in the Scotch Song, who had

Neither Pot nor Pan,
But four bare Legs together;

for I had a House tolerably furnished, for an ordinary Man, before. No thanks to Dad, who I understand was very much pleased with his politick Management. And I have since learn'd that there are other old Curmudgeons (*so called*) besides him, who have this Trick, to marry their Daughters, and yet keep what they might well spare, till they can keep it no longer: But this by way of Digression; *A Word to the Wise is enough.*

I soon saw that with Care and Industry we might live tolerably easy, and in Credit with our Neighbours: But my Wife had a strong Inclination to be a *Gentlewoman*. In Consequence of this, my old-fashioned Looking-Glass was one Day broke, as she said, *No Mortal could tell which way.* However, since we could not be without a Glass in the Room, *My Dear*, says she, *we may as well buy a large fashionable One that Mr.* Such-a-one *has to sell; it will cost but little more than a common Glass, and will be much handsomer and more creditable.* Accordingly the Glass was bought, and hung against the Wall: But in a Week's time, I was made sensible by little and little, *that the Table was by no Means suitable to such a Glass.* And a more proper Table being procur'd, my Spouse, who was an excellent Contriver, inform'd me where we might have very handsome Chairs *in the Way*: And thus, by Degrees, I found all my old Furniture stow'd up in the Garret, and every thing below alter'd for the better.

Had we stopp'd here, we might have done well enough; but my Wife being entertain'd with *Tea* by the Good Women she visited, we could do no less than the like when they visited us; and so we got a *Tea-Table* with all its Appurtenances of *China* and *Silver.* Then my Spouse unfortunately overwork'd herself in washing the House, so that we could do no longer without a *Maid.* Besides this, it happened frequently, that when I came home at *One*, the Dinner was but just put in the Pot; for, *My Dear thought really it had been but Eleven*: At other Times when I came at the same Hour, *She wondered I would stay so long, for Dinner was ready and had waited for me these two Hours.* These Irregularities, occasioned by mistaking the Time, convinced me, that it was absolutely necessary *to buy a Clock*; which my Spouse observ'd, *was a great Ornament to the Room!* And lastly, to my Grief, she was frequently troubled with some Ailment or other, and nothing did her so much Good as *Riding*; And *these Hackney Horses were such wretched ugly Creatures, that*—I bought a very fine pacing Mare, which cost £20. And hereabouts Affairs have stood for some Months past.

I could see all along, that this Way of Living was utterly inconsistent with my Circumstances, but had not Resolution enough to help it. Till lately, receiving a very severe Dun, which mention'd the next Court, I began in earnest to project Relief. Last Monday my Dear went over the River, to see a Relation, and stay a Fortnight, because *she could not bear the Heat of the Town.* In the Interim, I have taken my Turn to make Alterations, *viz.* I have turn'd away the Maid, Bag and Baggage (for what should we do with a Maid, who have [except my Boy] none but our selves.) I have sold the fine Pacing Mare, and bought a good Milch Cow with £3 of the Money. I have dispos'd of the Tea-Table, and put a Spinning Wheel in its Place, which methinks *looks very pretty*: Nine empty Canisters I have stuff'd with Flax; and with some of the Money of the Tea-Furniture, I have bought a Set of Knitting-Needles; for to tell you a Truth, which I would have go no farther, *I begin to want Stockings*. The stately Clock I have transform'd into an Hour-Glass, by which I gain'd a good round Sum; and one of the Pieces of the old Looking-Glass, squar'd and fram'd, supplies the Place of the Great One, which I have convey'd into a Closet, where it may possibly remain some years. In short, the Face of Things is quite changed; and I am mightily pleased when I look at my Hour-Glass, *what an Ornament it is to the Room*. I have paid my Debts, and find Money in my Pocket. I expect my Dame home next Friday, and as your Paper is taken in at the House where she is, I hope the Reading of this will prepare her Mind for the above surprizing Revolutions. If she can conform to this new Scheme of Living, we shall be the happiest Couple perhaps in the Province, and, by the Blessing of God, may soon be in thriving Circumstances. I have reserv'd the great Glass, because I know her Heart is set upon it. I will allow her when she comes in, to be taken suddenly ill with the *Headach*, the *Stomach-ach*, *Fainting-Fits*, or whatever other Disorder she may think more proper; and she may retire to Bed as soon as she pleases: But if I do not find her in perfect Health both of Body and Mind the next Morning, away goes the aforesaid Great Glass, with several other Trinkets I have no Occasion for, to the Vendue that very Day. Which is the irrevocable Resolution of, Sir,

Her loving Husband, and
Your very humble Servant,
Anthony Afterwit.

Postscript: *You know we can return to our former Way of Living, when we please, if* Dad *will be at the Expence of it.*

The Pennsylvania Gazette, JULY 10, 1732

CELIA SINGLE

My Correspondent Mrs. Celia, *must excuse my omitting those Circumstances of her Letter, which point at People* too plainly; *and content herself that I insert the rest as follows.*

Mr. Gazetteer,

I must needs tell you, that some of the Things you print do more Harm than Good; particularly I think so of my Neighbour the Tradesman's Letter in one of your late Papers, which has broken the Peace of several Families, by causing Difference between Men and their Wives: I shall give you here one Instance, of which I was an Eye and Ear Witness.

Happening last *Wednesday* Morning to be in at Mrs. *C—ss's*, when her Husband return'd from Market, among other Things which he had bought, he show'd her some Balls of Thread. *My Dear*, says he, *I like mightily those Stockins which I yesterday saw Neighbour* Afterwit *knitting for her Husband, of Thread of her own Spinning: I should be glad to have some such Stockins my self: I understand that your Maid* Mary *is a very good Knit-*

ter, and seeing this Thread in Market, I have bought it, that the Girl may make a Pair or two for me. Mrs. *Careless* was just then at the Glass, dressing her Head; and turning about with the Pins in her Mouth, *Lord, Child,* says she, *are you crazy? What Time has* Mary *to knit? Who must do the Work, I wonder, if you set her to Knitting?* Perhaps, my Dear, *says he,* you have a mind to knit 'em yourself; I remember, when I courted you, I once heard you say you had learn'd to knit of your Mother. *I knit Stockins for you,* says she, *not I truly, There are poor Women enough in Town, that can knit; if you please you may employ them.* Well, but my Dear, *says he,* you know a penny sav'd is a penny got, a pin a day is a groat a year, every little makes a mickle, and there is neither Sin nor Shame in Knitting a pair of Stockins; why should you express such a mighty Aversion to it? As to *poor* Women, you know we are not People of Quality, we have no Income to maintain us, but what arises from my Labour and Industry; methinks you should not be at all displeas'd, if you have an Opportunity to get something as well as my self. *I wonder,* says she, *how you can propose such a thing to me; did not you always tell me you would maintain me like a Gentlewoman? If I had married* Capt. ——, *he would have scorn'd even to mention Knitting of Stockins.* Prithee, *says he, (a little nettled)* what do you tell me of your Captains? If you could have had him: I suppose you would; or perhaps you did not very well like him: If I did promise to maintain you like a Gentlewoman, I suppose 'tis time enough for that when you know how to behave like one; mean while 'tis your Duty to help make me able. How long d'ye think I can maintain you at your present Rate of Living? *Pray,* says she, (somewhat fiercely, and dashing the Puff into the Powder-Box) *don't use me after this Manner, for I assure you I won't bear it. This is the Fruit of your poison* News-papers; *there shall come no more here, I promise you.* Bless us, *says he,* what an unaccountable thing is this! Must a Tradesman's Daughter, and the Wife of a Tradesman, necessarily and instantly be a Gentlewoman? You had no Portion; I am forc'd to work for a Living; if you are too great to do the like, there's the Door, go and live upon your Estate, if you can find it; in short, I don't desire to be troubled w'ye.—What Answer she made, I cannot tell; for knowing that a Man and his Wife are apt to quarrel more violently when before Strangers, than when by themselves, I got up and went out hastily: But I understood from *Mary*, who came to me of an Errand in the Evening, that they dined together pretty peaceably, (the Balls of Thread that had caused the Difference, being thrown into the Kitchen Fire) of which I was very glad to hear.

I have several times in your Paper seen severe Reflections upon us Women, for Idleness and Extravagance, but I do not remember to have once seen any such Animadversions upon the Men. If I were dispos'd to be censorious, I could furnish you with Instances enough: I might mention Mr. *Billiard*, who spends more than he earns, at the Green Table; and would have been in Jail long since, were it not for his industrious Wife: Mr. *Husselcap*, who often all day long leaves his Business for the rattling of Halfpence in a certain Alley: Mr. *Finikin*, who has seven different Suits of fine Cloaths, and wears a Change every Day, while his Wife and Children sit at home half naked: Mr. *Crownhim*, who is always dreaming over the Checquer-board, and cares not how the World goes, so he gets the Game: Mr. *T'otherpot* the Tavern-haunter; Mr. *Bookish*, the everlasting Reader; Mr. Tweedledum, Mr. *Toot-a-toot*, and several others, who are mighty diligent at any thing beside their Business. I say, if I were dispos'd to be censorious, I might mention all these, and more; but I hate to be thought a Scandalizer of my Neighbours, and therefore forbear. And for your part, I would advise you, for the future, to entertain your Readers with something else besides People's Reflections upon one another; for remember, that there are Holes enough to be pick'd in your Coat as well as others; and those that are affronted by the Satyrs you may publish, will not consider so much who *wrote*, as who *printed*: Take not this Freedom amiss, from

Your Friend and Reader,
Celia Single.

The Pennsylvania Gazette, JULY 24, 1732

ON CENSURE OR BACKBITING

Impia sub dulci melle venena latent.   Ovid.
Naturam expellas furcâ licet, usq; recurret.   Hor.

There is scarce any one Thing so generally spoke against, and at the same time so universally practis'd, as *Censure* or *Backbiting.* All Divines have condemn'd it, all Religions have forbid it, all Writers of Morality have endeavour'd to discountenance it, and all Men hate it at all Times, except only when they have Occasion to make use of it. For my part, after having frankly declar'd it as my Opinion, that the general Condemnation it meets with, proceeds only from a Consciousness in most People that they have highly incurr'd and deserv'd it, I shall in a very fearless impudent Manner take upon me to oppose the universal Vogue of Mankind in all Ages, and say as much in Behalf and Vindication of this decry'd Virtue, as the usual Vacancy in your Paper will admit.

I have call'd it a Virtue, and shall take the same Method to prove it such, as we commonly use to demonstrate any other Action or Habit to be a Virtue, that is, by shewing its Usefulness, and the great Good it does to Society. What can be said to the contrary, has already been said by every body; and indeed it is so little to the purpose, that any body may easily say it: But the Path I mean to tread, has hitherto been trod by no body; if therefore I should meet with the Difficulties usual in tracing new Roads, and be in some Places a little at loss, the Candour of the Reader will the more readily excuse me.

The first Advantage I shall mention, arising from the free Practice of *Censure* or *Backbiting*, is, that it is frequently the Means of preventing powerful, politick, ill-designing Men, from growing too popular for the Safety of a State. Such Men are always setting their best Actions to view, in order to obtain Confidence and Trust, and establish a Party: They endeavour to shine with false or borrow'd Merit, and carefully conceal their real Demerit: (that they fear to be evil spoken of is evident from their striving to cover every Ill with a specious Pretence;) But all-examining CENSURE, with her hundred Eyes and her thousand Tongues, soon discovers and as speedily divulges in all Quarters, every the least Crime or Foible that is a part of their true Character. This clips the Wings of their Ambition, weakens their Cause and Party, and reduces them to the necessity of dropping their pernicious Designs, springing from a violent Thirst of Honour and Power; or, if that Thirst is unquenchable, they are oblig'd to enter into a Course of true Virtue, without which real Grandeur is not to be attained.

Again, the common Practice of *Censure* is a mighty Restraint upon the Actions of every private Man; it greatly assists our otherwise weak Resolutions of living virtuously. *What will the World say of me, if I act thus?* is often a Reflection strong enough to enable us to resist the most powerful Temptation to Vice or Folly. This preserves the Integrity of the Wavering, the Honesty of the Covetous, the Sanctity of some of the Religious, and the Chastity of all Virgins. And, indeed, when People once become regardless of *Censure*, they are arrived to a Pitch of Impudence little inferior to the Contempt of all Laws humane and divine.

The common Practice of *Censure* is also exceedingly serviceable, in helping a Man to *the Knowledge of himself*; a piece of Knowledge highly necessary for all, but acquired by very few, because very few sufficiently regard and value the Censure past by others on their Actions. There is hardly such a Thing as a Friend, sincere or rash enough to acquaint us freely with our Faults; nor will any but an Enemy tell us of what we have done amiss, *to our Faces*; and Enemies meet with little Credit in such Cases, for we believe they speak from Malice and Illwill: Thus we might always live in the blindest Ignorance of our own Folly, and, while every body reproach'd us in their Hearts, might think our Conduct irreproachable: But Thanks be to Providence, (that has given every Man a natural Inclination to backbite his Neighbour) we now hear of many Things said *of* us, that we shall never hear said *to* us; (for out of Goodwill to us, or Illwill to those that have spoken ill of us, every one is willing enough to tell us how we are censur'd by others,) and we have the Advantage of mending our Manners accordingly.

Another vast Benefit arising from the common Practice of *Backbiting*, is, that it helps exceedingly to a thorough *Knowledge of Mankind*, a Science the most useful of all Sciences. Could we come to know no Man of whom we had not a particular Experience, our Sphere of Knowledge of this Sort would certainly be narrow and confined, and yet at the same Time must probably have cost us very dear. For the crafty tricking Villain would have a vast Advantage over the honest undesigning Part of Men, when he might cheat and abuse almost every one he dealt with, if none would take the Liberty to characterize him among their Acquaintance behind his Back.

Without saying any more in its Behalf, I am able to challenge all the Orators or Writers in the World, to show (with solid Reason) that the few trifling Inconveniencies attending it, bear any Proportion to these vast Benefits! And I will venture to assert to their Noses, that nothing would be more absurd or pernicious than a Law against Backbiting, if such a Law could possibly take Effect; since it would undoubtedly be the greatest Encouragement to Vice that ever Vice met with, and do more towards the encreasing it, than would the Abolishing of all other Laws whatsoever.

I might likewise have mentioned the Usefulness of *Censure* in Society, as it is a certain and an equal Punishment for such Follies and Vices as the common Laws either do not sufficiently punish, or have provided no Punishment for. I might have observed, that were it not for this, we should find the Number of some Sorts of Criminals increased to a Degree sufficient not only to infest, but even to overthrow all good and civil Conversation: But it is endless to enumerate every particular Advantage arising from this glorious Virtue! A Virtue, which whoever exerts, must have the largest Share of Publick Spirit and Self-denial, the highest Benevolence and Regard to the Good of others; since in This he entirely sacrifices his own Interest, making not only the Persons he accuses, but all that hear him, his Enemies; for all that deserve Censure (which are by far the greatest Number) hate the Censorious;

> *That dangerous Weapon, Wit,*
> *Frightens a Million when a few you hit:*
> *Whip but a Cur as you ride thro' a Town,*

And strait his Fellow Curs the Quarrel own:
Each Knave or Fool that's conscious of a Crime,
Tho' he scapes now, looks for't another time.

A Virtue! decry'd by all that fear it, but a strong Presumption of the Innocence of them that practise it; for they cannot be encouraged to offend, from the least Prospect of Favour or Impunity; their Faults or Failings will certainly meet with no Quarter from others. And whoever practises the Contrary, always endeavouring to excuse and palliate the Crimes of others, may rationally be suspected to have some secret darling Vice, which he hopes will be excused him in return. A Virtue! which however ill People may load it with the opprobrious Names of *Calumny, Scandal,* and *Detraction,* and I know not what; will still remain a Virtue, a bright, shining, solid Virtue, of more real Use to Mankind than all the other Virtues put together; and indeed, is the Mother or the Protectress of them all, as well as the Enemy, the Destructress of all kinds of Vice. A Virtue, innately, necessarily, and essentially so; for —— But, dear Reader, large Folio Volumes closely written, would scarce be sufficient to contain all the Praises due to it. I shall offer you at present only one more convincing Argument in its Behalf, *viz.* that you would not have had the Satisfaction of seeing this Discourse so agreeably short as I shall make it, were it not for the just Fear I have of incurring your *Censure,* should I continue to be troublesome by extending it to a greater Length.

The Pennsylvania Gazette, SEPTEMBER 7, 1732

ALICE ADDERTONGUE

Mr. Gazetteer,

I was highly pleased with your last Week's Paper upon SCAN-DAL, as the uncommon Doctrine therein preach'd is agreeable both to my Principles and Practice, and as it was published very seasonably to reprove the Impertinence of a Writer in the foregoing Thursday's *Mercury*, who at the Conclusion of one of his silly Paragraphs, laments, forsooth, that the *Fair Sex* are so peculiarly guilty of this enormous Crime: Every Blockhead, ancient and modern, that could handle a Pen, has I think taken upon him to cant in the same senseless Strain. If to *scandalize* be really a *Crime*, what do these Puppies mean? They describe it, they dress it up in the most odious frightful and detestable Colours, they represent it as the worst of Crimes, and then roundly and charitably charge the whole Race of Womankind with it. Are they not then guilty of what they condemn, at the same time that they condemn it? If they accuse us of any other Crime, they must necessarily *scandalize* while they do it: But to *scandalize* us with being guilty of *Scandal*, is in itself an egregious Absurdity, and can proceed from nothing but the most consummate Impudence in Conjunction with the most profound Stupidity.

This, supposing, as they do, that to scandalize is a Crime; which you have convinc'd all reasonable People, is an Opinion absolutely erroneous. Let us leave then these Ideot Mock-Moralists, while I entertain you with some Account of my Life and Manners.

I am a young Girl of about thirty-five, and live at present with my Mother. I have no Care upon my Head of getting a Living, and therefore find it my Duty as well as Inclination, to exercise my Talent at *Censure*, for the Good of my Country folks. There was, I am told, a certain generous Emperor, who if a Day had passed over his Head, in which he had conferred no Benefit on any Man, used to say to his Friends, in Latin, *Diem perdidi*, that is, it seems, *I have lost a Day*. I believe I should make use of the same Expression, if it were possible for a Day to pass in which I had not, or miss'd, an Opportunity to scandalize somebody: But, Thanks be praised, no such Misfortune has befel me these dozen Years.

Yet, whatever Good I may do, I cannot pretend that I first entred into the Practice of this Virtue from a Principle of Publick Spirit; for I remember that when a Child, I had a violent Inclination to be ever talking in my own Praise, and being continually told that it was ill Manners, and once severely whipt for it, the confin'd Stream form'd itself a new Channel, and I began to speak for the future in the Dispraise of others. This I found more agreeable to Company, and almost as much so to my self: For what great Difference can there be, between putting your self up, or putting your Neighbour down? *Scandal*, like other Virtues, is in part its own Reward, as it gives us the Satisfaction of making our selves appear better than others, or others no better than ourselves.

My Mother, good Woman, and I, have heretofore differ'd upon this Account. She argu'd that Scandal spoilt all good Conversation, and I insisted that without it there could be no such Thing. Our Disputes once rose so high, that we parted Tea-Table, and I concluded to entertain my Acquaintance in the Kitchin. The first Day of this Separation we both drank Tea at the same Time, but she with her Visitors in the Parlor. She would not hear of the least Objection to any one's Character, but began a new sort of Discourse in some such queer philosophical Manner as this: *I am mightily pleas'd sometimes*, says she, *when I observe and consider that the World is not so bad as People out of humour imagine it to be. There is something amiable, some good Quality or other in every body. If we were only to speak of People that are least respected, there is* such a one *is very dutiful to her Father, and methinks has a fine Set of Teeth*; such a one *is very respectful to her Husband*; such a one *is very kind to her poor Neighbours, and besides has a very handsome Shape*; such a one *is always ready to serve a Friend, and in my Opinion there is not a Woman in Town that has a more agreeable Air and Gait*. This fine kind of Talk, which lasted near half an Hour, she concluded by saying, *I do not doubt but every one of you have made the like Observations, and I should be glad to have the Conversation continu'd upon this Subject*. Just at that Juncture I peep'd in at the Door, and never in my Life before saw such a Set of simple vacant Countenances; they looked somehow neither glad, nor sorry, nor angry, nor pleas'd, nor indifferent, nor attentive; but (excuse the Simile) like so many blue wooden images of Rie Doe. I in the Kitchin had already begun a ridiculous Story of Mr. ——'s Intrigue with his Maid, and his Wife's Behaviour upon the Discovery; at some Passages we laugh'd heartily, and one of the gravest of Mama's Company, without making any Answer to her Discourse, got up *to go and see what the Girls were so merry about*: She was follow'd by a Second, and shortly after by a Third, till at last the old Gentlewoman found herself quite alone, and being convinc'd that her Project was impracticable, came her self and finish'd her Tea with us; ever since which *Saul also has been among the Prophets*, and our Disputes lie dormant.

By Industry and Application, I have made my self the Center of all the *Scandal* in the Province, there is little stirring but I hear of it. I began the World with this Maxim, *That no Trade can subsist without Returns*; and accordingly, whenever I receiv'd a good Story, I endeavour'd to give two or a better in the Room of it. My Punctuality in this Way of Dealing gave such Encouragement, that it has procur'd me an incredible deal of Business, which without Diligence and good Method it would be impossible for me to go through. For besides the Stock of Defamation thus naturally flowing in upon me, I practice an Art by which I can pump Scandal out of People that are the least enclin'd that way. Shall I discover my Secret? Yes; to let it die with me would be inhuman.—If I have never heard Ill of some Person, I always impute it to defective Intelligence; *for there are none without their Faults, no not one.* If she is a Woman, I take the first Opportunity to let all her Acquaintance know I have heard that one of the handsomest or best Men in Town has said something in Praise either of her Beauty, her Wit, her Virtue, or her good Management. If you know any thing of Humane Nature, you perceive that this naturally introduces a Conversation turning upon all her Failings, past, present, and to come. To the same purpose, and with the same Success, I cause every Man of Reputation to be praised before his Competitors in Love, Business, or Esteem on Account of any particular Qualification. Near the Times of *Election*, if I find it necessary, I commend every Candidate before some of the opposite Party, listning attentively to what is said of him in answer: (But Commendations in this latter Case are not always necessary, and should be used judiciously;) of late Years I needed only observe what they said of one another freely; and having for the Help of Memory taken Account of all Information & Accusations received, whoever pe-ruses my Writings after my Death, may happen to think, that during a certain Term, the People of *Pennsylvania* chose into all their Offices of Honour and Trust, the veriest Knaves, Fools and Rascals in the whole Province. The Time of Election used to be a busy Time with me, but this Year, with Concern I speak it, People are grown so good-natur'd, so intent upon mutual Feasting and friendly Entertainment, that I see no Prospect of much Employment from that Quarter.

I mention'd above, that without good Method I could not go thro' my Business: In my Father's Life-time I had some Instruction in Accompts, which I now apply with Advantage to my own Affairs. I keep a regular Set of Books, and can tell at an Hour's Warning how it stands between me and the World. In my *Daybook* I enter every Article of Defamation as it is trans-acted; for Scandals *receiv'd in*, I give Credit; and when I pay them out again, I make the Persons to whom they respectively relate *Debtor*. In my *Journal*, I add to each Story by way of Improvement, such probable Circumstances as I think it will bear; and in my *Ledger* the whole is regularly posted.

I suppose the Reader already condemns me in his Heart, for this particular of *adding Circumstances*; but I justify that part of my Practice thus. 'Tis a Principle with me, that none ought to have a greater Share of Reputation than they really deserve; if they have, 'tis an Imposition upon the Publick: I know it is every one's Interest, and therefore believe they endeavour, to conceal *all* their Vices and Follies; and I hold, that those People are *extraordinary* foolish or careless who suffer a *Fourth* of their Failings to come to publick Knowledge: Taking then the common Prudence and Imprudence of Mankind in a Lump, I suppose none suffer above *one Fifth* to be discovered: Therefore when I hear of any Person's Misdoing, I think I keep within Bounds if in relating it I only make it *three times* worse than it is; and I reserve to my self the Privilege of charging them with one Fault in four, which, for aught I know, they may be entirely innocent of. You see there are but few so careful of doing Justice as my self; what Reason then have Mankind to complain of *Scandal?* In a general way, the worst that is said of us is only half what *might* be said, if all our Faults were seen.

But alas, two great Evils have lately befaln me at the same time; an extream Cold that I can scarce speak, and a most terrible Toothach that I dare hardly open my Mouth: For some Days past I have receiv'd ten Stories for one I have paid; and I am not able to ballance my Accounts without your Assistance. I have long thought that if you would make your Paper a Vehicle of Scandal, you would double the Number of your Subscribers. I send you herewith Account of 4 *Knavish Tricks*, 2 *crackt M—n-ds*, 5 *Cu–ld-ms*, 3 *drub'd Wives*, and 4 *Henpeck'd Husbands*, all within this Fortnight; which you may, as Articles of News, deliver to the Publick; and if my Toothach continues, shall send you more; being, in the mean time,

Your constant Reader,

Alice Addertongue.

I thank my Correspondent, Mrs. Addertongue *for her Good-Will; but desire to be excus'd inserting the Articles of News she has sent me; such Things being in Reality* no News at all.

The Pennsylvania Gazette, September 12, 1732

ON CONSTANCY

Hi mores hæc duri immota CATONIS
Secta fuit, servare modum, finemque tenere,
Naturamque sequi, patriæque impendere vitam. LUCAN.

When I have sometimes observ'd Men of Wit and Learning, in Spite of their excellent natural and acquir'd Qualifications, fail of obtaining that Regard and Esteem with Mankind, which their Inferiors in point of Understanding frequently arrive at, I have, upon a slight Reflection, been apt to think, that it was owing to the ill Judgment, Malice, or Envy of their Acquaintance: But of late two or three flagrant Instances of this kind have put me upon thinking and deliberating more maturely, and I find within the Compass of my Observation the greatest part of those fine Men have been ruined for want of *CONSTANCY*, a Virtue never too highly priz'd, and whose true Worth is by few rightly understood.

A Man remarkably wavering and inconstant, who goes through with no Enterprize, adheres to no Purpose that he has resolv'd on, whose Courage is surmounted by the most trifling Obstacles, whose Judgment is at any time byass'd by his Fears, whose trembling and disturb'd Imagination will at every Turn suggest to him Difficulties and Dangers that actually have no Existence, and enlarge those that have; A Man, I say, of this Stamp, whatever natural and acquir'd Qualities he may have, can never be a truly useful Member of a Common-wealth, a sincere or amiable Friend, or a formidable Enemy; and when he is once incapable of bearing either of these Characters, 'tis no Wonder he is contemn'd and disregarded by Men of all Ranks and Conditions.

Without Steadiness or Perseverance no Virtue can long subsist; and however honest and well-meaning a Man's Principles may be, the Want of this is sufficient to render them ineffectual, and useless to himself or others. Nor can a Man pretend to enjoy or impart the lasting Sweets of a strict and glorious Friendship, who has not Solidity enough to despise the malicious Misrepresentations frequently made use of to disturb it, and which never fail of Success where a mutual Esteem is not founded upon the solid Basis of Constancy and Virtue. An Intimacy of this sort, contracted by chance, or the Caprice of an unstable Man, is liable to the most violent Shocks, and even an intire Ruin, from very trifling Causes. Such a Man's Incapacity for Friendship, makes all that know his Character absolutely indifferent to him: His known Fickleness of Temper renders him too inconsiderable to be fear'd as a Foe, or caress'd as a Friend.

I may venture to say there never was a Man eminently famous but what was distinguish'd by this very Qualification; and few if any can live comfortably even in a private Life without it; for a Man who has no End in View, no Design to pursue, is like an irresolute Master of a Ship at Sea, that can fix upon no one Port to steer her to, and consequently can call not one Wind favourable to his Wishes.

'Tis by his firm and unshaken Adherence to his Country's Cause, his constant Bravery in her Defence, and his burying himself but in her Ruins, that the rigid and severe *Cato* shines thro' those admirable Lines of *Lucan*, of which my Motto is a part, superior to the learn'd and eloquent *Cicero*, the great and majestick *Pompey*, or the mighty and invincible *Cæsar* himself. This is alone what could move the Poet to set him in Competition with the Gods themselves, and will transmit him down to latest Posterity with the highest Veneration and Honour.

To come nearer to our own Times; 'Tis the extraordinary Constancy of *Charles* XII. of *Sweden*, which makes up the most admirable and inimitable Part of his Character: His severe and impartial Distribution of Justice in his Army, and that fierce and resolute Speech with which he broke up his Council, *Gentlemen, I have resolved never to engage in an unjust War, but never to finish one that is founded upon Justice and Right, but by the Destruction of my Enemies*: these and such like Instances of his Steadiness and Perseverance in the Pursuit of Justice, have deservedly made him esteem'd the Wonder of his Age.

King *Charles* II. of *England*, was doubtless a Man of great Understanding: His acquir'd Qualities far surpass'd those of *Cromwell*, and his natural Talents at least equal'd them: He came to rule over a People, formidable to all *Europe* for their Bravery, and exceedingly prepossessed in his Favour; he had learn'd to bear Misfortune by many Years Exile, and numerous Hazards and Difficulties: With these Advantages how great and glorious might he have made his Reign, by the Happiness, Content and Security of his People! 'Tis however undeniable, that the *English* never were less happy, or less regarded by their Neighbours, than during his Reign. The Reason is obvious; his Inconstancy and Indolence laid him open to every trifling Project, every self-interested Scheme, that an avaritious or revengeful Minister or Mistress could suggest to him for their own sinister Ends. 'Tis this has given many Occasion to think, that he acted thro'out his whole Reign upon no Principles and Maxims, and had no one Design in View.

Cromwel came to the supreme Authority with few of these Advantages, and against the Will of the whole Nation, except a few Fanaticks in the Army; but his constant and resolute Carriage, which was the Effect of his keeping one principal End in view, surmounted all Obstacles: 'Twas this, and this alone, which rais'd him so far above the Malice of his Enemies, or the Expectation of his Friends; and gain'd him that high Character from a judicious Historian, *That never Man chose his Party with more Judgment, and executed his Designs with more Constancy and Vigour.* By virtue of this Constancy the *English* Nation under him arriv'd to that Pitch of Grandeur, as to become a Terror and Dread to their Enemies, and the greatest Protection to their Allies. 'Tis this steady Perseverance that render'd him the Center of the different Factions and Interests in which *England* was at that time embroil'd, that secur'd his former Friends and Adherents to his Interest, and deter'd his Foes from attempting to undermine his Authority.

The Pennsylvania Gazette, APRIL 4, 1734

THE ART OF SAYING LITTLE
IN MUCH

mplification, or the Art of saying *Little in Much*, seems to be principally studied by the Gentlemen Retainers to the Law. 'Tis highly useful when they are to speak at the Bar; for by its Help, they talk a great while, and appear to say a great deal, when they have really very little to say. But 'tis principally us'd in Deeds and every thing they write. You must abridge their Performances to understand them; and when you find how little there is in a Writing of vast Bulk, you will be as much surpriz'd as a Stranger at the Opening of a *Pumpkin*.

It is said, that in the Reign of *William* the Conqueror, the Conveyance of a large Estate, might be made in about half a dozen short Lines; which was nevertheless in every Respect sufficiently authentick. For several Hundred Years past, Conveyances and Writings in the Law have been continually encreasing in Bulk, and when they will come to their full Growth, no Man knows: For the Rule, *That every thing past and present ought to be express'd, and every thing future provided for*, (tho' one would think a large Writing might be made by it) does not serve to confine us at present; since all those things are not only to be express'd, but may (by the Modern License) be express'd by all the *different Words* we can think of. Probably the Invention of Printing, which took from the Scribes great Part of their former Employment, put them on the Contrivance of making up by a Multitude of Words, what they wanted in real Business; hence the plain and strong Expression, *shall be his own,* is now swoln into, *shall and may at all Times hereafter forever, and so from time to time, freely, quietly and peaceably, have, hold and enjoy, &c.* The Lawyer, in one of *Steele's* Comedies, instructs his Pupil, that *Tautology* is the first, second, and third Parts of his Profession, that is to say, *the whole of it*: And adds, *That he hopes to see the Time, when it will require as much Parchment to convey a Piece of Land as will cover it.* That time perhaps is not far off: For I am told, that the Deeds belonging to the Title of some small Lotts, (which have gone thro' several Hands) are nearly sufficient for the Purpose.

But of all the Writings I have ever seen, for the Multiplicity, Variety, Particularity, and prodigious Flow of Expression, none come up to the Petition of *Dermond O Folivey*, an Attorney of the Kingdom of *Ireland*: As the Petition is curious in itself, and may serve as a Precedent for young Clerks, when they would acquire a proper Stile in their Performances, I shall give it to the Publick entire, as follows.

To the Right Honourable *Sir William Asten*, Knight, and
Lord Judge of Assize of the *Munster* Circuit.
The humble Petition *of* Dermond O Folivey *a well
and most accomplished Gentleman.*

'Most humbly, and most submissively, and most obediently, and most dutifully, by shewing, and expressing, and declaring to your Lordship, that whereby, and whereas, and wherein, the most major, and most greater, and most bigger, and the most stronger Part of the most best, and the most ablest, and the most mightiest Sort of the People of the Barony of *Torrough* and County of *Kerry*, finding, and knowing, and certifying themselves, both hereafter, and the Time past, and now, and then, and at the present time, to be very much oppressed, and distressed, and overcharged in all Taxes, and Quit-rents, and other Levies, and accidental Applotments, and Collections, and Gatherings-together in the Barony of *Torrough* and County of *Kerry* aforesaid, And for the future Prevention of all, and every such, henceforth, hereafter, heretofore, and for the time to come, and now, and then, and at this time, and forever, the aforesaid most major, and most bigger, and most better, and most stronger Part of the most best, and most ablest, and most mightiest Sort of the People of *Torrough* and County of *Kerry* aforesaid, HATH appointed, nominated, constituted, ordained, declared, elected, and made me Mr. *Dermond O Folivey* to solicite, and make mention to your Lordship, looking upon me now, and then, and there, and here, the said Mr. *Dermond O Folivey*, to be the fittest, the most mightiest, and the most ablest, and the most best, and the most accomplished, and the most eloquentest Spokesman within the said Barony and County, their granded, and well beloved, and well bestowed, and better merited Agent and Sollicitor, to represent Oppression, and Suppression, and Extortion, for all such, and for all much, and whereof, and whereby, and whereupon, your Petitioner fairly, and finely, and honestly, and ingeniously, and deservedly appointed, nominated, constituted, and ordained, and elected, and approved, and made choice of me the said Mr. *Dermond O Folivey* as an Agent and Sollicitor, to undergo, and overgo, and under-run, and over-run, and manage this much, big, and mighty Service.

'These are therefore to will, and to shall be, now, and then, and there, and at this time, and at the time past, and heretofore, and formerly, and at the present, and forever, the humble, and special, and important, and mighty, and irrefatigable Request of me, your Petitioner and Sollicitor-General aforesaid; THAT your Lordship will be pleased, and satisfied, and resolved, to grant, and give, and deliver, and bestow, upon me Mr. *Dermond O Folivey*, your before recited, and nominated Petitioner and Sollicitor-General aforesaid, an Order and Judgment, and Warrant, and Authority of Preference to my Lord *Kerry*, and Mr. *Henry Punceby*, Esq; and Justice of the Peace and Quorum, or to any four or five or more or less, or either or neither of them, now, and then, and there, and here, and any where, and every where, and somewhere, and no-where, to call and bring, and fetch, and carry, before him, or them, or either of them, or neither, or both, such Party or Parties as they shall imagine, and conceive, and consider, and suppose, and assent, and esteem, and think fit, and meet, and necessary, and decent, and convenient, all, and every, and either, or neither of them, to call, to examine, and call to a strict Account; and that Part, and most Part, Extortion; and then, and there, when, and where, and whether, to establish, and elect, and direct, and impower, and authorize all such, and all much, Bailiffs, and under Receivers, and Collectors and Gatherers-together of Money, as your Petitioner did, or do, or have, or had, or shall, or will, or may, or might, or should, or could, or ought to chuse, or pitch upon with, and punctually to desire my self Mr. *Dermond O Folivey* that they, them, and these, and every, and either, and neither of them, that shall, and did, and have, and do, and will him in Peace, and Unity, and Amity, and Concord, and Tranquility, henceforth, and for the time to come, and hereafter, and for the time past, and not past, and the time present, and now, and for everlasting; and especially not to molest, or trouble, or hinder, or disturb, or hurt, or meddle with the Petitioner, my self, Mr. *Dermond O Folivey*, in his Possession of 72 Acres of Land in *Gertogolinmore* in the Barony of *Torrough* and County of *Kerry*.'

Given, and granted, and dated, and signed, and sealed by my own Hand and with my own Hand, and for my own Hand, and under my own Hand and Seal this — Day of — Anno Dom. —— } Mr. *Dermond O Folivey.*

The Pennsylvania Gazette, JUNE 17, 1736

THE DRINKER'S DICTIONARY

Nothing more like a Fool than a drunken Man. POOR RICHARD

'Tis an old Remark, that Vice always endeavours to assume the Appearance of Virtue: Thus Covetousness calls itself *Prudence*; *Prodigality* would be thought *Generosity*; and so of others. This perhaps arises hence, that Mankind naturally and universally approve Virtue in their Hearts, and detest Vice; and therefore, whenever thro' Temptation they fall into a Practice of the latter, they would if possible conceal it from themselves as well as others, under some other Name than that which properly belongs to it.

But DRUNKENNESS is a very unfortunate Vice in this respect. It bears no kind of Similitude with any sort of Virtue, from which it might possible borrow a Name; and is therefore reduc'd to the wretched Necessity of being express'd by distant round-about Phrases, and of perpetually varying those Phrases, as often as they come to be well understood to signify plainly that A MAN IS DRUNK.

Tho' every one may possibly recollect a Dozen at least of the Expressions us'd on this Occasion, yet I think no one who has not much frequented Taverns would imagine the number of them so great as it really is. It may therefore surprize as well as divert the sober Reader, to have the Sight of a new Piece, lately communicated to me, entitled

The DRINKERS DICTIONARY.

A

He is Addled,

He's casting up his Accounts,

He's Afflicted,

He's in his Airs.

B

He's Biggy,

 Bewitch'd,

 Block and Block,

 Boozy,

 Bowz'd,

 Been at Barbadoes,

 Piss'd in the Brook,

 Drunk as a Wheel-Barrow,

 Burdock'd,

 Buskey,

 Buzzey,

Has Stole a Manchet out of

 the Brewer's Basket,

His Head is full of Bees,

Has been in the Bibbing Plot,

Has drank more than he has bled,

He's Bungey,

As Drunk as a Beggar,

He sees the Bears,

He's kiss'd black Betty,

He's had a Thump over the

 Head with Sampson's

 Jawbone,

He's Bridgey.

C

He's Cat,

 Cagrin'd,

 Capable,

 Cramp'd,

 Cherubimical,

 Cherry Merry,

 Wamble Crop'd,

 Crack'd,

 Concern'd,

 Half Way to Concord,

Has taken a Chirriping-Glass,

 Got Corns in his Head,

 A Cup too much,

 Coguy,

 Copey,

He's heat his Copper,
He's Crocus,
    Catch'd,
He cuts his Capers,
He's been in the Cellar,
He's in his Cups,
    Non Compos,
    Cock'd,
    Curv'd,
    Cut,
    Chipper,
    Chickery,
    Loaded his Cart,
He's been too free with the
    Creature,
Sir Richard has taken off his
    Considering Cap,
He's Chap-fallen,

D
He's Disguiz'd,
He's got a Dish,
    Kill'd his Dog,
    Took his Drops,
It is a Dark Day with him,
He's a Dead Man,

Has Dipp'd his Bill,
He's Dagg'd,
He's seen the Devil,

E
He's Prince Eugene,
    Enter'd,
    Wet both Eyes,
    Cock Ey'd,
    Got the Pole Evil,
    Got a brass Eye,
    Made an Example,
He's Eat a Toad & half for
    Breakfast.
    In his Element,

F
He's Fishey,
    Fox'd,
    Fuddled,
    Sore Footed,
    Frozen,
    Well in for 't,
    Owes no Man a Farthing,
    Fears no Man,
    Crump Footed,
    Been to France,

Flush'd,
Froze his Mouth,
Fetter'd,
Been to a Funeral,
His Flag is out,
Fuzl'd,
Spoke with his Friend,
Been at an Indian Feast.

G

He's Glad,
Groatable,
Gold-headed,
Glaiz'd,
Generous,
Booz'd the Gage,
As Dizzy as a Goose,
Been before George,
Got the Gout,
Had a Kick in the Guts,
Been with Sir John Goa,
Been at Geneva,
Globular,
Got the Glanders.

H

Half and Half,

Hardy,
Top Heavy,
Got by the Head,
Hiddey,
Got on his little Hat,
Hammerish,
Loose in the Hilts,
Knows not the way Home,
Got the Hornson,
Haunted with Evil Spirits,
Has taken Hippocrates
    grand Elixir,

I

He's Intoxicated,

J

He's Jolly,
Jagg'd,
Jambl'd,
Going to Jerusalem,
Jocular,
Been to Jerico,
Juicy.

K

He's a King,

Clips the King's English,
Seen the French King,
The King is his Cousin,
Got Kib'd Heels,
Knapt,
Het his Kettle.

L

He's in Liquor,
Lordly,
He makes Indentures with
his Leggs,
Well to Live,
Light,
Lappy,
Limber,

M

He sees two Moons,
Merry,
Middling,
Moon-Ey'd,
Muddled,
Seen a Flock of Moons,
Maudlin,
Mountous,

Muddy,
Rais'd his Monuments,
Mellow,

N

He's eat the Cocoa Nut,
Nimptopsical,
Got the Night Mare,

O

He's Oil'd,
Eat Opium,
Smelt of an Onion,
Oxycrocium,
Overset,

P

He drank till he gave up his
Half-Penny,
Pidgeon Ey'd,
Pungey,
Priddy,
As good conditioned as a
Puppy,
Has scalt his Head Pan,
Been among the Philistines,
In his Prosperity,

He's been among the
    Philippians,
He's contending with
    Pharaoh,
    Wasted his Paunch,
He's Polite,
    Eat a Pudding
      Bagg,

Q
He's Quarrelsome,

R
He's Rocky,
    Raddled,
    Rich,
    Religious,
    Lost his Rudder,
    Ragged,
    Rais'd,
    Been too free with Sir
      Richard,
    Like a Rat in Trouble.

S
He's Stitch'd,
    Seafaring,

In the Sudds,
    Strong,
    Been in the Sun,
    As Drunk as David's Sow,
    Swampt,
His Skin is full,
He's Steady,
He's Stiff,
He's burnt his Shoulder,
He's got his Top Gallant Sails out,
    Seen the yellow Star,
    As Stiff as a Ring-bolt,
    Half Seas over,
    His Shoe pinches him,
    Staggerish,
    It is Star-light with him,
    He carries too much Sail,
    Stew'd,
    Stubb'd,
    Soak'd,
    Soft,
Been too free with Sir John Strawberry,
He's right before the Wind with
    all his Studding Sails out,
Has Sold his Senses.

T

He's Top'd,
> Tongue-ty'd,
>
> Tann'd,
>
> Tipium Grove,
>
> Double Tongu'd,
>
> Topsy Turvey,
>
> Tipsey,

Has Swallow'd a Tavern Token,

He's Thaw'd,

He's in a Trance,

He's Trammel'd,

V

He makes Virginia Fence,
> Valiant,
>
> Got the Indian Vapours,

W

The Malt is above the Water,

He's Wise,

He's Wet,

He's been to the Salt Water,

He's Water-soaken,

He's very Weary,
> Out of the Way.

The Phrases in this Dictionary are not (like most of our Terms of Art) borrow'd from Foreign Languages, neither are they collected from the Writings of the Learned in our own, but gather'd wholly from the modern Tavern-Conversation of Tiplers. I do not doubt but that there are many more in use; and I was even tempted to add a new one my self under the Letter B, to with *Brutify'd*: But upon Consideration, I fear'd being guilty of Injustice to wit, the Brute Creation, if I represented Drunkenness as a beastly Vice, since, 'tis well-known, that the Brutes are in general a very sober sort of People.

The Pennsylvania Gazette, JANUARY 13, 1736/7

ADVICE TO A YOUNG TRADESMAN, WRITTEN BY AN OLD ONE

To My Friend *A. B.*

As you have desired it of me, I write the following Hints, which have been of Service to me, and may, if observed, be so to you.

Remember that TIME is Money. He that can earn Ten Shillings a Day by his Labor, and goes abroad, or sits idle one half of that Day, tho' he spends but Sixpence during his Diversion or Idleness, ought not to reckon That the only Expence; he has really spent or rather thrown away Five Shillings besides.

Remember that CREDIT is Money. If a Man lets his Money lie in my Hands after it is due, he gives me the Interest, or so much as I can make of it during that Time. This amounts to a considerable Sum where a Man has good and large Credit, and makes good Use of it.

Remember that Money is of the prolific generating Nature. Money can beget Money, and its Offspring can beget more, and so on. Five Shillings turn'd, is *Six*: Turn'd again, 'tis Seven and Three Pence; and so on 'til it becomes an Hundred Pound. The more there is of it, the more it produces every Turning, so that the Profits rise quicker and quicker. He that kills a breeding Sow, destroys all her Offspring to the thousandth Generation. He that murders a Crown, destroys all that it might have produc'd, even Scores of Pounds.

Remember that Six Pounds a Year is but a Groat a Day. For this little Sum (which may be daily wasted either in Time or Expence unperceiv'd) a Man of Credit may, on his own Security have the constant Possession and Use of an Hundred Pounds. So much in Stock briskly turn'd by an industrious Man, produces great Advantage.

Remember this Saying; *That the good Paymaster is Lord of another Man's Purse.* He that is known to pay punctually and exactly to the Time he promises, may at any Time, and on any Occasion, raise all the Money his Friends can spare. This is sometimes of great Use: Therefore never keep borrow'd Money an Hour beyond the Time you promis'd, lest a Disappointment shuts up your Friends Purse forever.

The most trifling Actions that affect a Man's Credit, are to be regarded. The Sound of your Hammer at Five in the Morning or Nine at Night, heard by a Creditor, makes him easy Six Months longer. But if he sees you at a Billiard Table, or hears your Voice in a Tavern, when you should be at Work, he sends for his Money the next Day. Finer Cloaths than he or his Wife wears, or greater Expence in any particular than he affords himself, shocks his Pride, and he duns you to humble you. Creditors are a kind of People, that have the sharpest Eyes and Ears, as well as the best Memories of any in the World.

Good-natur'd Creditors (and such one would always chuse to deal with if one could) feel Pain when they are oblig'd to ask for Money. Spare 'em that Pain, and they will love you. When you receive a Sum of Money, divide it among 'em in Proportion to your Debts. Don't be asham'd of paying a small Sum because you owe a greater. Money, more or less, is always welcome; and your Creditor had rather be at the Trouble of receiving Ten Pounds voluntarily brought him, tho' at ten different Times or Payments, than be oblig'd to go ten Times to demand it before he can receive it in a Lump. It shews, besides, that you are mindful of what you owe; it makes you appear a careful as well as an honest Man; and that still encreases your Credit.

Beware of thinking all your own that you possess, and of living accordingly. 'Tis a mistake that many People who have Credit fall into. To prevent this, keep an exact Account for some Time of both your Expences and your Incomes. If you take the Pains at first to mention Particulars, it will have this good Effect; you will discover how wonderfully small trifling Expences mount up to large Sums, and will discern what might have been, and may for the future be saved, without occasioning any great Inconvenience.

In short, the Way to Wealth, if you desire it, is as plain as the Way to Market. It depends chiefly on two Words, INDUSTRY and FRUGALITY; *i.e.* Waste neither Time nor Money, but make the best Use of both. He that gets all he can honestly, and saves all he gets (necessary Expences excepted) will certainly become RICH; If that Being who governs the World, to whom all should look for a Blessing on their Honest Endeavours, doth not in his wise Providence otherwise determine.

Philadelphia,
B. Franklin and D. Hall,
at the New-Printing-Office, 1748

RULES PROPER TO BE OBSERVED IN TRADE

I.   Endeavour to be perfect in the calling you are engaged in; and be assiduous in every part thereof; INDUSTRY being the natural means of acquiring *wealth, honour,* and *reputation*; as *idleness* is of *poverty, shame,* and *disgrace.*

II.   Lay a good foundation in regard to principle: Be sure not wilfully to over-reach, or deceive your neighbour; but keep always in your eye the golden rule of *doing as you would be done unto.*

III.   Be strict in discharging all legal debts: Do not evade your creditors by any shuffling arts, in giving notes under your hand, only to defer payment; but, if you have it in your power, discharge all debts when they become due. Above all, when you are straitened for want of money, be cautious of taking it up at an high interest. This has been the ruin of many, therefore endeavour to avoid it.

IV.   Endeavour to be as much in your shop, or warehouse, or in whatever place your business properly lies, as possibly you can: Leave it not to servants to transact, for customers will not regard them as yourself; they generally think they shall not be so well served: Besides, mistakes may arise by the negligence, or inexperience, of servants; and therefore, your presence will prevent, probably, the loss of a good customer.

V.   Be complaisant to the *meanest*, as well as greatest: You are as much
     obliged to use good manners for a farthing, as a pound; the one
     demands it from you, as well as the other.

VI. Be not too talkative, but speak as much as is necessary to recom-
     mend your goods, and always observe to keep within the rules of
     decency. If customers slight your goods, and undervalue them,
     endeavour to convince them of their mistake, if you can, but not
     affront them: Do not be pert in your answers, but with patience
     hear, and with meekness give an answer; for if you affront in a
     small matter, it may probably hinder you from a future good cus-
     tomer. They may think that you are dear in the articles they want;
     but, by going to another, may find it not so, and probably may
     return again; but if you behave rude and affronting, there is no
     hope either of returning, or their future custom.

VII. Take great care in keeping your accounts well: Enter every thing
     necessary in your books with neatness and exactness; often state
     your accounts, and examine whether you gain, or lose; and carefully
     survey your stock, and inspect into every particular of your affairs.

VIII. Take care, as much as you can, whom you trust: Neither take nor
     give long credit; but, at the farthest, annually settle your accounts.
     Deal at the fountain head for as many articles as you can; and, if it
     lies in your power, for ready money: This method you will find to be
     the most profitable in the end. Endeavour to keep a proper assort-
     ment in your way, but not over-stock yourself. Aim not at making
     a great figure in your shop, in unnecessary ornaments, but let it be
     neat and useful: Too great an appearance may rather prevent, than

engage customers. Make your *business* your pleasure, and other entertainments will only appear necessary for relaxation therefrom.

IX.   Strive to maintain a *fair character* in the world: That will be the best means for advancing your credit, gaining you the most flourishing trade, and enlarging your fortune. Condescend to no mean action, but add a lustre to trade, by keeping up to the dignity of your nature.

The Pennsylvania Gazette, FEBRUARY 20, 1749/50

RULES FOR MAKING ONESELF A DISAGREEABLE COMPANION

RULES, *by the Observation of which, a Man of Wit and Learning may nevertheless make himself a* DISAGREEABLE *Companion.*

Your Business is to *shine*; therefore you must by all means prevent the shining of others, for their Brightness may make yours the less distinguish'd. To this End,

1.   If possible engross the whole Discourse; and when other Matter fails, talk much of your-self, your Education, your Knowledge, your Circumstances, your Successes in Business, your Victories in Disputes, your own wise Sayings and Observations on particular Occasions, &c. &c. &c.

2. If when you are out of Breath, one of the Company should seize the Opportunity of saying something; watch his Words, and, if possible, find somewhat either in his Sentiment or Expression, immediately to contradict and raise a Dispute upon. Rather than fail, criticise even his Grammar.

3. If another should be saying an indisputably good Thing; either give no Attention to it; or interrupt him; or draw away the Attention of others; or, if you can guess what he would be at, be quick and say it before him; or, if he gets it said, and you perceive the Company pleas'd with it, own it to be a good Thing, and withal remark that it had been said by *Bacon*, *Locke*, *Bayle*, or some other eminent Writer; thus you deprive him of the Reputation he might have gain'd by it, and gain some yourself, as you hereby show your great Reading and Memory.

4. When modest Men have been thus treated by you a few times, they will chuse ever after to be silent in your Company; then you may shine on without Fear of a Rival; rallying them at the same time for their Dullness, which will be to you a new Fund of Wit.

Thus you will be sure to please *yourself.* The polite Man aims at pleasing *others*, but you shall go beyond him even in that. A Man can be present only in one Company, but may at the same time be absent in twenty. He can please only where he *is*, you where-ever you are *not*.

The Pennsylvania Gazette, NOVEMBER 15, 1750

THE WAY TO WEALTH

AS CLEARLY SHOWN IN THE PREFACE OF AN OLD PENNSYLVANIA

ALMANAC, ENTITLED, "POOR RICHARD IMPROVED."

COURTEOUS READER,

I HAVE heard, that nothing gives an author so great pleasure as to find his works respectfully quoted by others. Judge, then, how much I must have been gratified by an incident I am going to relate to you. I stopped my horse lately, where a great number of people were collected at an auction of merchants' goods. The hour of the sale not being come, they were conversing on the badness of the times; and one of the company called to a plain, clean, old man, with white locks, "Pray, Father Abraham, what think you of the times? Will not these heavy taxes quite ruin the country? How shall we ever be able to pay them? What would you advise us to?" Father Abraham stood up, and replied, "If you would have my advice, I will give it you in short; for *A word to the wise is enough*, as Poor Richard says." They joined in desiring him to speak his mind, and gathering round him, he proceeded as follows.

"Friends," said he, "the taxes are indeed very heavy, and, if those laid on by the government were the only ones we had to pay, we might more easily discharge them; but we have many others, and much more grievous to some of us. We are taxed twice as much by our idleness, three times as much by our pride, and four times as much by our folly; and from these taxes the commissioners cannot ease or deliver us, by allowing an abatement. However, let us hearken to good advice, and something may be done for us; *God helps them that help themselves*, as Poor Richard says.

"I. It would be thought a hard government, that should tax its people one-tenth part of their time, to be employed in its service; but idleness taxes many of us much more; sloth, by bringing on diseases, absolutely shortens life. *Sloth, like rust, consumes faster than labor wears; while the used key is always bright*, as Poor Richard says. *But dost thou love life, then do not squander time, for that is the stuff life is made of*, as Poor Richard says. How much more than is necessary do we spend in sleep, forgetting, that *The sleeping fox catches no poultry*, and that *There will be sleeping enough in the grave*, as Poor Richard says.

"*If time be of all things the most precious, wasting time must be*, as Poor Richard says, *the greatest prodigality;* since, as he elsewhere tells us, *Lost time is never found again; and what we call time enough, always proves little enough.* Let us then up and be doing, and doing to the purpose; so by diligence shall we do more with less perplexity. *Sloth makes all things difficult, but industry all easy; and He that riseth late must trot all day, and shall scarce overtake his business at night; while Laziness travels so slowly, that Poverty soon overtakes him. Drive thy business, let not that drive thee; and Early to bed, and early to rise, makes a man healthy, wealthy, and wise*, as Poor Richard says.

"So what signifies wishing and hoping for better times? We may make these times better, if we bestir ourselves. *Industry need not wish, and he that lives upon hopes will die fasting. There are no gains without pains; then help, hands, for I have no lands;* or, if I have, they are smartly taxed. *He that hath a trade hath an estate; and he that hath a calling, hath an office of profit and honor,* as Poor Richard says; but then the trade must be worked at, and the calling followed, or neither the estate nor the office will enable us to pay our taxes. If we are industrious, we shall never starve; for, *At the working man's house hunger looks in, but dares not enter.* Nor will the bailiff or the constable enter, for *Industry pays debts, while despair increaseth them.* What though you have found no treasure, nor has any rich relation left you a legacy, *Diligence is the mother of good luck, and God gives all things to industry. Then plough deep while sluggards sleep, and you shall have corn to sell and to keep.* Work while it is called to-day, for you know not how much you may be hindered to-morrow. *One to-day is worth two to-morrows,* as Poor Richard says; and further, *Never leave that till to-morrow, which you can do to-day.* If you were a servant, would you not be ashamed that a good master should catch you idle? Are you then your own master? Be ashamed to catch yourself idle, when there is so much to be done for yourself, your family, your country, and your king. Handle your tools without mittens; remember, that *The cat in gloves catches no mice,* as Poor Richard says. It is true there is much to be done, and perhaps you are weak-handed; but stick to it steadily, and you will see great effects; for *Constant dropping wears away stones;* and *By diligence and patience the mouse ate in two the cable;* and *Little strokes fell great oaks.*

"Methinks I hear some of you say, 'Must a man afford himself no leisure?' I will tell thee, my friend, what Poor Richard says, *Employ thy time well, if thou meanest to gain leisure; and, since thou art not sure of a minute, throw not away an hour.* Leisure is time for doing something useful; this leisure the diligent man will obtain, but the lazy man never; for *A life of leisure and a life of laziness are two things. Many, without labor, would live by their wits only, but they break for want of stock;* whereas industry gives comfort, and plenty, and respect. *Fly pleasures, and they will follow you. The diligent spinner has a large shift; and now I have a sheep and a cow, everybody bids me good morrow.*

"II. But with our industry we must likewise be steady, settled, and careful, and oversee our own affairs with our own eyes, and not trust too much to others; for, as Poor Richard says,

> *I never saw an oft-removed tree.*
> *Nor yet an oft-removed family,*
> *That throve so well as those that settled be.*

And again, *Three removes are as bad as a fire;* and again, *Keep thy shop, and thy shop will keep thee;* and again, *If you would have your business done, go; if not, send.* And again,

> *He that by the plough would thrive,*
> *Himself must either hold or drive.*

And again, *The eye of a master will do more work than both his hands;* and again, *Want of care does us more damage than want of knowledge;* and again, *Not to oversee workmen, is to leave them your purse open.* Trusting too much to others' care is the ruin of many; for *In the affairs of this world men are saved, not by faith, but by the want of it;* but a man's own care is profitable; for, *If you would have a faithful servant, and one that you like, serve yourself. A little neglect may breed great mischief; for want of a nail the shoe was lost; for want of a shoe the horse was lost; and for want of a horse the rider was lost, being overtaken and slain by the enemy; all for want of a little care about a horse-shoe nail.*

"III. So much for industry, my friends, and attention to one's own business; but to these we must add frugality, if we would make our industry more certainly successful. A man may, if he knows not how to save as he gets, keep his nose all his life to the grindstone, and die not worth a groat at last. *A fat kitchen makes a lean will;* and

> *Many estates are spent in the getting,*
> *Since women for tea forsook spinning and knitting,*
> *And men for punch forsook hewing and splitting.*

If you would be wealthy, think of saving as well as of getting. The Indies have not made Spain rich, because her outgoes are greater than her incomes.

"Away then with your expensive follies, and you will not then have so much cause to complain of hard times, heavy taxes, and chargeable families; for

> *Women and wine, game and deceit,*
> *Make the wealth small and the want great.*

And further, *What maintains one vice would bring up two children.* You may think, perhaps, that a little tea, or a little punch now and then, diet a little more costly, clothes a little finer, and a little entertainment now and then, can be no great matter; but remember, *Many a little makes a mickle.* Beware of little expenses; *A small leak will sink a great ship,* as Poor Richard says; and again, *Who dainties love, shall beggars prove;* and moreover, *Fools make feasts, and wise men eat them.*

"Here you are all got together at this sale of fineries and knick-knacks. You call them *goods;* but, if you do not take care, they will prove *evils* to some of you. You expect they will be sold cheap, and perhaps they may for less than they cost; but, if you have no occasion for them, they must be dear to you. Remember what Poor Richard says; *Buy what thou hast no need of, and ere long thou shalt sell thy necessaries.* And again, *At a great pennyworth pause a while.* He means, that perhaps the cheapness is apparent only, and not real; or the bargain, by straitening thee in thy business, may do thee more harm than good. For in another place he says, *Many have been ruined by buying good pennyworths.* Again, *It is foolish to lay out money in a purchase of repentance;* and yet this folly is practised every day at auctions, for want of minding the Almanac. Many a one, for the sake of finery on the back, have gone with a hungry belly and half-starved their families. *Silks and satins, scarlet and velvets, put out the kitchen fire,* as Poor Richard says.

"These are not the necessaries of life; they can scarcely be called the conveniences; and yet, only because they look pretty, how many want to have them! By these, and other extravagances, the genteel are reduced to poverty, and forced to borrow of those whom they formerly despised, but who, through industry and frugality, have maintained their standing; in which case it appears plainly, that *A ploughman on his legs is higher than a gentleman on his knees,* as Poor Richard says. Perhaps they have had a small estate left them, which they knew not the getting of; they think, *It is day, and will never be night;* that a little to be spent out of so much is not worth minding; but *Always taking out of the meal-tub, and never putting in, soon comes to the bottom,* as Poor Richard says; and then, *When the well is dry, they know the worth of water.* But this they might have known before, if they had taken his advice. *If you would know the value of money, go and try to borrow some; for he that goes a borrowing goes a sorrowing,* as Poor Richard says; and indeed so does he that lends to such people, when he goes to get it in again. Poor Dick further advises, and says,

> *Fond pride of dress is sure a very curse;*
> *Ere fancy you consult, consult your purse.*

And again, *Pride is as loud a beggar as Want, and a great deal more saucy.* When you have bought one fine thing, you must buy ten more, that your appearance may be all of a piece; but Poor Dick says, *It is easier to suppress the first desire, than to satisfy all that follow it.* And it is as truly folly for the poor to ape the rich, as for the frog to swell in order to equal the ox.

> *Vessels large may venture more,*
> *But little boats should keep near shore.*

It is, however, a folly soon punished; for, as Poor Richard says, *Pride that dines on vanity, sups on contempt. Pride breakfasted with Plenty, dined with Poverty, and supped with Infamy.* And, after all, of what use is this pride of appearance, for which so much is risked, so much is suffered? It cannot promote health, nor ease pain; it makes no increase of merit in the person; it creates envy; it hastens misfortune.

"But what madness must it be to *run in debt* for these superfluities? We are offered by the terms of this sale, six months' credit; and that, perhaps, has induced some of us to attend it, because we cannot spare the ready money, and hope now to be fine without it. But, ah! think what you do when you run in debt; you give to another power over your liberty. If you cannot pay at the time, you will be ashamed to see your creditor; you will be in fear when you speak to him; you will make poor, pitiful, sneaking excuses, and, by degrees, come to lose your veracity, and sink into base, downright lying; for *The second vice is lying, the first is running in debt*, as Poor Richard says; and again, to the same purpose, *Lying rides upon Debt's back;* whereas a free-born Englishman ought not to be ashamed nor afraid to see or speak to any man living. But poverty often deprives a man of all spirit and virtue. *It is hard for an empty bag to stand upright.*

"What would you think of that prince, or of that government, who should issue an edict forbidding you to dress like a gentleman or gentlewoman, on pain of imprisonment or servitude? Would you not say that you were free, have a right to dress as you please, and that such an edict would be a breach of your privileges, and such a government tyrannical? And yet you are about to put yourself under such tyranny, when you run in debt for such dress! Your creditor has authority, at his pleasure, to deprive you of your liberty, by confining you in gaol till you shall be able to pay him. When you have got your bargain, you may, perhaps, think little of payment; but, as Poor Richard says, *Creditors have better memories than debtors; creditors are a superstitious sect, great observers of set days and times.* The day comes round before you are aware, and the demand is made before you are prepared to satisfy it; or, if you bear your debt in mind, the term, which at first seemed so long, will, as it lessens, appear extremely short. Time will seem to have added wings to his heels as well as his shoulders. *Those have a short Lent, who owe money to be paid at Easter.* At present, perhaps, you may think yourselves in thriving circumstances, and that you can bear a little extravagance without injury; but

> *For age and want save while you may;*
> *No morning sun lasts a whole day.*

Gain may be temporary and uncertain, but ever, while you live, expense is constant and certain; and *It is easier to build two chimneys, than to keep one in fuel*, as Poor Richard says; so, *Rather go to bed supperless, than rise in debt.*

> *Get what you can, and what you get hold;*
> *'Tis the stone that will turn all your lead into gold.*

And, when you have got the Philosopher's stone, sure you will no longer complain of bad times, or the difficulty of paying taxes.

"IV. This doctrine, my friends, is reason and wisdom; but, after all, do not depend too much upon your own industry, and frugality, and prudence, though excellent things; for they may all be blasted, without the blessing of Heaven; and, therefore, ask that blessing humbly, and be not uncharitable to those that at present seem to want it, but comfort and help them. Remember, Job suffered, and was afterwards prosperous.

"And now, to conclude, *Experience keeps a dear school, but fools will learn in no other*, as Poor Richard says, and scarce in that; for, it is true, *We may give advice, but we cannot give conduct.* However, remember this, *They that will not be counselled, cannot be helped;* and further, that, *If you will not hear Reason, she will surely rap your knuckles*, as Poor Richard says."

Thus the old gentleman ended his harangue. The people heard it, and approved the doctrine; and immediately practised the contrary, just as if it had been a common sermon; for the auction opened, and they began to buy extravagantly. I found the good man had thoroughly studied my Almanacs, and digested all I had dropped on these topics during the course of twenty-five years. The frequent mention he made of me must have tired any one else; but my vanity was wonderfully delighted with it, though I was conscious that not a tenth part of the wisdom was my own, which he ascribed to me, but rather the gleanings that I had made of the sense of all ages and nations. However, I resolved to be the better for the echo of it; and, though I had at first determined to buy stuff for a new coat, I went away resolved to wear my old one a little longer. Reader, if thou wilt do the same, thy profit will be as great as mine. I am, as ever, thine to serve thee,

Richard Saunders.

THE EPHEMERA

You may remember, my dear Friend, that when we lately spent that happy Day in the delightful Garden and sweet Society of the Moulin Joli, I stopt a little in one of our Walks, and staid some time behind the Company. We had been shewn numberless Skeletons of a kind of little Fly, called an Ephemere all whose successive Generations we were told were bred and expired within the Day. I happen'd to see a living Company of them on a Leaf, who appear'd to be engag'd in Conversation.—You know I understand all the inferior Animal Tongues: my too great Application to the Study of them is the best Excuse I can give for the little Progress I have made in your charming Language. I listened thro' Curiosity to the Discourse of these little Creatures; but as they in their national Vivacity spoke three or four together, I could make but little of their Discourse. I found, however, by some broken Expressions that I caught now & then, they were disputing warmly the Merit of two foreign Musicians, one a *Cousin*, the other a *Mosketo*; in which Dispute they spent their time seemingly as regardless of the Shortness of Life, as if they had been Sure of living a Month. Happy People! thought I, you live certainly under a wise, just, and mild Government; since you have no public Grievances to complain of, nor any Subject of Contention but the Perfection or Imperfection of foreign Music. I turned from them to an old grey-headed one, who was single on another Leaf, & talking to himself. Being amus'd with his Soliloquy, I have put it down in writing in hopes it will likewise amuse her to whom I am so much indebted for the most pleasing of all Amusements, her delicious Company and her heavenly Harmony.

"It was, says he, the Opinion of learned Philosophers of our Race, who lived and flourished long before my time, that this vast World, the *Moulin Joli*, could not itself subsist more than 18 Hours; and I think there was some Foundation for that Opinion, since by the apparent Motion of the great Luminary that gives Life to all Nature, and which in my time has evidently declin'd considerably towards the Ocean at the End of our Earth, it must then finish its Course, be extinguish'd in the Waters that surround us, and leave the World in Cold and Darkness, necessarily producing universal Death and Destruction. I have lived seven of these Hours; a great Age; being no less than 420 minutes of Time. How very few of us continue So long.—I have seen Generations born, flourish and expire. My present Friends are the Children and Grandchildren of the friends of my Youth, who are now, also, no more! And I must soon follow them; for by the Course of Nature, tho' still in Health, I cannot expect to live above 7 or 8 Minutes longer. What now avails all my Toil and Labor in amassing Honey-Dew on this Leaf, which I cannot live to enjoy! What the political Struggles I have been engag'd in for the Good of my Compatriotes, Inhabitants of this Bush, or my philosophical Studies for the Benefit of our Race in general! For in Politics *what can Laws do without Morals*.* Our present Race of Ephemeres will in a Course of Minutes, become corrupt like those of other and older Bushes, and consequently as wretched. And in Philosophy how small our Progress! Alas, *Art is long and Life is short*!†—My Friends

Quid leges sine moribus. Hor.
†Hippocrates.

would comfort me with the Idea of a Name they Say I shall leave behind me; and they tell me I have *lived long enough, to Nature and to Glory;*‡—But what will Fame be to an Ephemere who no longer exists? And what will become of all History in the 18th Hour, when the World itself, even the whole *Moulin Joli* shall come to its End, and be buried in universal Ruin?— To me, after all my eager Pursuits, no solid Pleasures now remain, but the Reflection of a long Life spent in meaning well, the sensible Conversation of a few good Lady-Ephemeres, and now and then a kind Smile and a Tune from the ever-amiable BRILLANTE."

PASSY SEPT 20, 1778

‡Cæsar.

THE ELYSIAN FIELDS

M. FRANKLIN TO MADAME HELVÉTIUS

Vexed by your barbarous resolution, announced so positively last evening, to remain single all your life in respect to your dear husband, I went home, fell on my bed, and, believing myself dead, found myself in the Elysian Fields.

I was asked if I desired to see anybody in particular. Lead me to the home of the philosophers.—There are two who live nearby in the garden: they are very good neighbors, and close friends of each other. —Who are they?—Socrates and H——.—I esteem them both prodigiously; but let me see first H——, because I understand a little French, but not one word of Greek. He received me with great courtesy, having known me for some time, he said, by the reputation I had there. He asked me a thousand things about the war, and about the present state of religion, liberty, and the government in France.—You ask nothing then of your dear friend Madame H——; nevertheless she still loves you excessively and I was at her place but an hour ago. Ah! said he, you make me remember my former felicity. —But it is necessary to forget it in order to be happy here. During several of the early years, I thought only of her. Finally I am consoled. I have taken another wife. The most like her that I could find. She is not, it is true, so completely beautiful, but she has as much good sense, a little more of Spirit, and she loves me infinitely. Her continual study is to please me; and she has actually gone to hunt the best Nectar and the best Ambrosia in order to regale me this evening; remain with me and you will see her. I perceive, I said, that your old friend is more faithful than you: for several good offers have been made her, all of which she has refused. I confess to you that I myself have loved her to the point of distraction; but she was hard-hearted to my regard, and has absolutely rejected me for love of you. I pity you, he said, for your bad fortune; for truly she is a good and beautiful woman and very loveable. But the Abbé de la R——, and the Abbé M——, are they not still sometimes at her home? Yes, assuredly, for she has not lost a single one of your friends. If you had won over the Abbé M—— (with coffee and cream) to speak for you, perhaps you would have succeeded; for he is a subtle logician like Duns Scotus or St. Thomas; he places his arguments in such good order that they become nearly irresistible. Also, if the Abbé de la R—— had been bribed (by some beautiful edition of an old classic) to speak against you, that would have been better: for I have always observed, that when he advises something, she has a very strong penchant to do the reverse.—At these words the new Madame H——entered with the Nectar: at which instant I recognized her to be Madame F——, my old American friend. I reclaimed to her. But she told me coldly, "I have been your good wife forty-nine years and four months, nearly a half century; be content with that. Here I have formed a new connection, which will endure to eternity."

Offended by this refusal of my Eurydice, I suddenly decided to leave these ungrateful spirits, to return to the good earth, to see again the sunshine and you. Here I am! Let us revenge ourselves.

DECEMBER 7, 1778

THE WHISTLE

I received my dear Friend's two Letters, one for Wednesday & one for Saturday. This is again Wednesday. I do not deserve one for to day, because I have not answered the former. But indolent as I am, and averse to Writing, the Fear of having no more of your pleasing Epistles, if I do not contribute to the Correspondance, obliges me to take up my Pen: And as M. B. has kindly sent me Word, that he sets out to-morrow to see you; instead of spending this Wednesday Evening as I have done its Name-sakes, in your delightful Company, I sit down to spend it in thinking of you, in writing to you, & in reading over & over again your Letters.

I am charm'd with your Description of Paradise, & with your Plan of living there. And I approve much of your Conclusion, that in the mean time we should draw all the Good we can from this World. In my Opinion we might all draw more Good from it than we do, & suffer less Evil, if we would but take care *not to give too much for our Whistles*. For to me it seems that most of the unhappy People we meet with are become so by Neglect of that Caution.

You ask what I mean? —You love Stories, and will excuse my telling you one of my self. When I was a Child of seven Years old, my Friends on a Holiday fill'd my Pocket with Halfpence. I went directly to a Shop where they sold Toys for Children; and being charm'd with the Sound of a Whistle that I met by the way, in the hands of another Boy, I voluntarily offer'd and gave all my Money for it. When I came home, whistling all over the House, much pleas'd with my Whistle, but disturbing all the Family, my Brothers, Sisters & Cousins, understanding the Bargain I had made, told me I had given four times as much for it as it was worth, put me in mind what good Things I might have bought with the rest of the Money, & laught at me so much for my Folly that I cry'd with Vexation; and the Reflection gave me more Chagrin than the Whistle gave me Pleasure.

This however was afterwards of use to me, the Impression continuing on my Mind; so that often when I was tempted to buy some unnecessary thing, I said to my self, *Do not give too much for the Whistle*; and I sav'd my Money.

As I grew up, came into the World, and observed the Actions of Men, I thought I met many *who gave too much for the Whistle.* —When I saw one ambitious of Court Favour, sacrificing his Time in Attendance on Levees, his Repose, his Liberty, his Virtue and perhaps his Friend, to obtain it; I have said to my self, *This Man gives too much for his Whistle.* —When I saw another fond of Popularity, constantly employing himself in political Bustles, neglecting his own Affairs, and ruining them by that Neglect, *He pays*, says I, *too much for his Whistle.* —If I knew a Miser, who gave up every kind of comfortable Living, all the Pleasure of doing Good to others, all the Esteem of his Fellow Citizens, & the Joys of benevolent Friendship, for the sake of Accumulating Wealth, *Poor man*, says I, *you pay too much for your Whistle.* —When I met with a Man of Pleasure, sacrificing every laudable Improvement of his Mind or of his Fortune, to mere corporeal Satisfactions, & ruining his Health in their Pursuit,

Mistaken man, says I, *you are providing Pain for your self instead of Pleasure, you pay too much for your Whistle.*—If I see one fond of Appearance, or fine Cloaths, fine Houses, fine Furniture, fine Equipages, all above his Fortune, for which he contracts Debts, and ends his Career in a Prison; *Alas,* says I, *he has paid too much for his Whistle.* —When I see a beautiful sweet-temper'd Girl, marry'd to an ill-natured Brute of a Husband; *What a Pity,* says I, *that she should pay so much for a Whistle!* —In short, I conceiv'd that great Part of the Miseries of Mankind were brought upon them by the false Estimates they had made of the Value of Things, and by their *giving too much for the Whistle.*

Yet I ought to have Charity for these unhappy People, when I consider that with all this Wisdom of which I am boasting, there are certain things in the World so tempting; for Example the Apples of King John, which happily are not to be bought, for if they were put to sale by Auction, I might very easily be led to ruin my self in the Purchase, and find that I had once more *given too much for the Whistle.*

Adieu, my dearest Friend, and believe me ever yours very sincerely and with unalterable Affection.

PASSY, NOVEMBER 10, 1779

DIALOGUE BETWEEN THE GOUT AND MR. FRANKLIN

MR. F.

Eh! oh! eh! What have I done to merit these cruel sufferings?

THE GOUT

Many things; you have ate and drank too freely, and too much indulged those legs of yours in their indolence.

MR. F.

Who is it that accuses me?

THE GOUT

It is I, even I, the Gout.

MR. F.

What! my enemy in person?

THE GOUT

No, not your enemy.

MR. F.

I repeat it, my enemy; for you would not only torment my body to death, but ruin my good name; you reproach me as a glutton and a tippler; now all the world, that knows me, will allow that I am neither the one nor the other.

THE GOUT

The world may think as it pleases; it is always very complaisant to itself, and sometimes to its friends; but I very well know that the quantity of meat and drink proper for a man who takes a reasonable degree of exercise, would be too much for another who never takes any.

MR. F.

I take—eh! oh!—as much exercise—eh!—as I can, Madam Gout. You know my sedentary state, and on that account, it would seem, Madam Gout, as if you might spare me a little, seeing it is not altogether my own fault.

THE GOUT

Not a jot; your rhetoric and your politeness are thrown away; your apology avails nothing. If your situation in life is a sedentary one, your amusements, your recreation, at least, should be active. You ought to walk or ride; or, if the weather prevents that, play at billiards. But let us examine your course of life. While the mornings are long, and you have leisure to go abroad, what do you do? Why, instead of gaining an appetite for breakfast by salutary exercise, you amuse yourself with books, pamphlets, or newspapers, which commonly are not worth the reading. Yet you eat an inordinate breakfast, four dishes of tea with cream, and one or two buttered toasts, with slices of hung beef, which I fancy are not things the most easily digested. Immediately afterwards you sit down to write at your desk, or converse with persons who apply to you on business. Thus the time passes till one, without any kind of bodily exercise. But all this I could pardon, in regard, as you say, to your sedentary condition. But what is your practice after dinner? Walking in the beautiful gardens of those friends with whom you have dined would be the choice of men of sense; yours is to be fixed down to chess, where you are found engaged for two or three hours! This is your perpetual recreation, which is the least eligible of any for a sedentary man, because, instead of accelerating the motion of the fluids, the rigid attention it requires helps to retard the circulation and obstruct internal secretions. Wrapt in the speculations of this wretched game, you destroy your constitution. What can be expected from such a course of living but a body replete with stagnant humours, ready to fall a prey to all kinds of dangerous maladies, if I, the Gout, did not occasionally bring you relief by agitating those humours, and so purifying or dissipating them? If it was in some nook or alley in Paris, deprived of walks, that you played a while at chess after dinner, this might be excusable; but the same taste prevails with you in Passy, Auteuil, Montmartre, or Sanoy, places where there are the finest gardens and walks, a pure air, beautiful women, and most agreeable and instructive conversation; all which you might enjoy by frequenting the walks. But these are rejected for this abominable game of chess. Fie, then, Mr. Franklin! But amidst my instructions, I had almost forgot to administer my wholesome corrections; so take that twinge—and that.

MR. F.

Oh! eh! oh! ohhh! As much instruction as you please, Madam Gout, and as many reproaches; but pray, Madam, a truce with your corrections!

THE GOUT

No, Sir, no, I will not abate a particle of what is so much for your good—therefore—

MR. F.

Oh! ehhh!—It is not fair to say I take no exercise, when I do very often, going out to dine and returning in my carriage.

THE GOUT

That, of all imaginable exercises, is the most slight and insignificant, if you allude to the motion of a carriage suspended on springs. By observing the degree of heat obtained by different kinds of motion, we may form an estimate of the quantity of exercise given by each. Thus, for example, if you turn out to walk in winter with cold feet, in an hour's time you will be in a glow all over; ride on horseback, the same effect will scarcely be perceived by four hours' round trotting; but if you loll in a carriage, such as you have mentioned, you may travel all day and gladly enter the last inn to warm your feet by a fire. Flatter yourself then no longer that half an hour's airing in your carriage deserves the name of exercise. Providence has appointed few to roll in carriages, while he has given to all a pair of legs, which are machines infinitely more commodious and serviceable. Be grateful, then, and make a proper use of yours. Would you know how they forward the circulation of your fluids in the very action of transporting you from place to place, observe when you walk that all your weight is alternately thrown from one leg to the other; this occasions a great pressure on the vessels of the foot, and repels their contents; when relieved, by the weight being thrown on the other foot, the vessels of the first are allowed to replenish, and by a return of this weight, this repulsion again succeeds; thus accelerating the circulation of the blood. The heat produced in any given time depends on the degree of this acceleration; the fluids are shaken, the humours attenuated, the secretions facilitated, and all goes well;

the cheeks are ruddy, and health is established. Behold your fair friend at Auteuil; a lady who received from bounteous nature more really useful science than half a dozen such pretenders to philosophy as you have been able to extract from all your books. When she honors you with a visit, it is on foot. She walks all hours of the day, and leaves indolence, and its concomitant maladies, to be endured by her horses. In this, see at once the preservative of her health and personal charms. But when you go to Auteuil, you must have your carriage, though it is no farther from Passy to Auteuil than from Auteuil to Passy.

MR. F.

Your reasonings grow very tiresome.

THE GOUT

I stand corrected. I will be silent and continue my office; take that, and that.

MR. F.

Oh! Ohh! Talk on, I pray you.

THE GOUT

No, no; I have a good number of twinges for you tonight, and you may be sure of some more tomorrow.

MR. F.

What, with such a fever! I shall go distracted. Oh! eh! Can no one bear it for me?

THE GOUT

Ask that of your horses; they have served you faithfully.

MR. F.

How can you so cruelly sport with my torments?

THE GOUT

Sport! I am very serious. I have here a list of offences against your own health distinctly written, and can justify every stroke inflicted on you.

MR. F.

Read it then.

THE GOUT

It is too long a detail; but I will briefly mention some particulars.

MR. F.

Proceed. I am all attention.

THE GOUT

Do you remember how often you have promised yourself, the following morning, a walk in the grove of Boulogne, in the garden de La Muette, or in your own garden, and have violated your promise, alleging, at one time, it was too cold, at another too warm, too windy, too moist, or what else you pleased; when in truth it was too nothing, but your insuperable love of ease?

MR. F.

That I confess may have happened occasionally, probably ten times in a year.

THE GOUT

Your confession is very far short of the truth; the gross amount is one hundred and ninety-nine times.

MR. F.

Is it possible?

THE GOUT

So possible, that it is fact; you may rely on the accuracy of my statement. You know M. Brillon's gardens, and what fine walks they contain; you know the handsome flight of an hundred steps which lead from the terrace above to the lawn below. You have been in the practice of visiting this amiable family twice a week, after dinner, and it is a maxim of your own, that "a man may take as much exercise in walking a mile up and down stairs, as in ten on level ground." What an opportunity was here for you to have had exercise in both these ways! Did you embrace it, and how often?

MR. F.

I cannot immediately answer that question.

THE GOUT

I will do it for you; not once.

MR. F.

Not once?

THE GOUT

Even so. During the summer you went there at six o'clock. You found the charming lady, with her lovely children and friends, eager to walk with you, and entertain you with their agreeable conversation; and what has been your choice? Why, to sit on the terrace, satisfying yourself with the fine prospect, and passing your eye over the beauties of the garden below, without taking one step to descend and walk about in them. On the contrary, you call for tea and the chess-board; and lo! you are occupied in your seat till nine o'clock, and that besides two hours' play after dinner; and then, instead of walking home, which would have bestirred you a little, you step into your carriage. How absurd to suppose that all this carelessness can be reconcilable with health, without my interposition!

MR. F.

I am convinced now of the justness of Poor Richard's remark, that "Our debts and our sins are always greater than we think for."

THE GOUT

So it is. You philosophers are sages in your maxims, and fools in your conduct.

MR. F.

But do you charge among my crimes, that I return in a carriage from M. Brillon's?

THE GOUT

Certainly; for having been seated all the while, you cannot object the fatigue of the day, and cannot want therefore the relief of a carriage.

MR. F.

What then would you have me do with my carriage?

THE GOUT

Burn it if you choose; you would at least get heat out of it once in this way; or if you dislike that proposal, here's another for you; observe the poor peasants who work in the vineyards and grounds about the villages of Passy, Auteuil, Chaillot, etc.; you may find every day among these deserving creatures four or five old men and women, bent and perhaps crippled by weight of years, and too long and too great labour. After a most fatiguing day these people have to trudge a mile or two to their smoky huts. Order your coachman to set them down. This is an act that will be good for your soul; and, at the same time, after your visit to the Brillons, if you return on foot, that will be good for your body.

MR. F.

Ah! how tiresome you are!

THE GOUT

Well, then, to my office; it should not be forgotten that I am your physician. There.

MR. F.

Ohhh! what a devil of a physician!

THE GOUT

How ungrateful you are to say so! Is it not I who, in the character of your physician, have saved you from the palsy, dropsy, and apoplexy? One or other of which would have done for you long ago, but for me.

MR. F.

I submit, and thank you for the past, but entreat the discontinuance of your visits for the future; for, in my mind, one had better die than be cured so dolefully. Permit me just to hint, that I have also not been unfriendly to *you*. I never feed physician or quack of any kind, to enter the list against you; if then you do not leave me to my repose, it may be said you are ungrateful too.

THE GOUT

I can scarcely acknowledge that as any objection. As to quacks, I despise them; they may kill you indeed, but cannot injure me. And as to regular physicians, they are at last convinced that the gout, in such a subject as you are, is no disease, but a remedy; and wherefore cure a remedy?—but to our business—there.

MR. F.

Oh! oh!—for Heaven's sake leave me! and I promise faithfully never more to play at chess, but to take exercise daily, and live temperately.

THE GOUT

I know you too well. You promise fair; but, after a few months of good health, you will return to your old habits; your fine promises will be forgotten like the forms of the last year's clouds. Let us then finish the account, and I will go. But I leave you with an assurance of visiting you again at a proper time and place; for my object is your good, and you are sensible now that I am your *real friend*.

THE HANDSOME AND
THE DEFORMED LEG

There are two Sorts of People in the World, who with equal Degrees of Health & Wealth and the other Comforts of Life, become, the one happy, the other unhappy. This arises very much from the different Views in which they consider Things, Persons, and Events; and the Effect of those different Views upon their own Minds.

In whatever Situation Men can be plac'd, they may find Conveniences and Inconveniences: In whatever Company, they may find Persons & Conversation more or less pleasing: At whatever Table they may meet with Meats and Drinks of better and worse Taste, Dishes better and worse dress'd: In whatever Climate they will find good and bad Weather: Under whatever Government, they may find good and bad Laws, and good and bad Administration of those Laws: In every Poem, or Work of Genius, they may see Faults and Beauties: In almost every Face & every Person, they may discover fine Features and Defects, good and bad Qualities. Under these Circumstances, the two Sorts of People above-mention'd fix their Attention, those who are to be happy, on the Conveniencies of Things, the pleasant Parts of Conversation, the well-dress'd & well-tasted Dishes, the Goodness of the Wines, the Fine Weather, &c. &c. &c. and enjoy all with Chearfulness: Those who are to be unhappy think and speak only of the contraries. Hence they are continually discontented themselves, and, by their Remarks sour the Pleasures of Society, offend personally many People, and make themselves every where disagreeable.

If this Turn of Mind was founded in Nature, such unhappy Persons would be the more to be pitied. But as the Disposition to criticise and be disgusted is perhaps taken up originally by Imitation, and unawares grown into a Habit, which tho at present strong, may nevertheless be cured, when those who have it are convinc'd of its bad Effects on their Felicity, I hope this little Admonition may be of Service to them, and put them on changing a Habit, which tho in the Exercise is chiefly an Act of Imagination, yet it has serious Consequences in Life, as it brings on real Griefs and Misfortunes: For, as many as are offended by, and nobody well loves this sort of People, no one shows them more than the most common Civility & Respect, and scarcely that; and this frequently puts them out of humour, and draws them into Disputes and Contentions. If they aim at obtaining some Advantage in Rank or Fortune, nobody wishes them Success, or will stir a Step, or speak a Word to favour their Pretensions. If they incur public Censure or Disgrace, no one will defend or excuse, and many join to aggravate their Misconduct, and render them completely odious.

If these People will not change this bad Habit, and condescend to be pleas'd with what is pleasing, without fretting themselves or others about the Contraries, it is good for others to avoid an Acquaintance with them, which is always disagreable, and sometimes very inconvenient, particularly when one finds one's self entangled in their Quarrels.

An old philosophical Friend of mine was grown from Experience very cautious in this particular and carefully shun'd any intimacy with such People. He had, like other Philosophers, a Thermometer to show him the Heat of the Weather, & a Barometer to mark when it was likely to prove good or bad; but there being no Instrument yet invented to discover at first Sight this unpleasing Disposition in a Person, he for that purpose made use of his Legs; one of which was remarkably handsome, the other by some Accident crooked and deform'd. If a Stranger, at the first Interview, regarded his ugly Leg more than his handsome one, he doubted him. If he spoke of it, and took no Notice of the handsome Leg, that was sufficient to determine my Philosopher to have no further Acquaintance with him.

Every body has not this two-legged Instrument, but every one, with a little Attention may observe Signs of that carping fault-finding Disposition; and take the same Resolution of avoiding the Acquaintance of those infected with it.

I therefore advise these critical, querulous, discontented, unhappy People, that if they wish to be loved & respected by others and happy in themselves, they should *leave off looking at the ugly Leg.*

NOVEMBER, 1780

THE FLIES

TO MADAME HELVÉTIUS

The Flies of the Apartments of Mr. Franklin request Permission to present their Respects to Madame Helvétius, & to express in their best Language their Gratitude for the Protection which she has been kind enough to give them,

Bizz izzzz ouizz a ouizzzz izzzzzzzz, &c.

We have long lived under the hospitable Roof of the said Good Man Franklin. He has given us free Lodgings; we have also eaten & drunk the whole Year at his Expense without its having cost us anything. Often, when his Friends & he have emptied a Bowl of Punch, he has left us a sufficient Quantity to intoxicate a hundred of us Flies. We have drunk freely of it, & after that we have made our Sallies, our Circles & our Cotillions very prettily in the Air of his Room, & have gaily consummated our little Loves under his Nose. In short, we should have been the happiest People in the World, if he had not permitted a Number of our declared Enemies to remain at the top of his Wainscoting, where they spread their Nets to catch us, & tore us pitilessly to pieces. People of a Disposition both subtle & ferocious, abominable Combination! You, most excellent Woman, had the goodness to order that all these Assassins with their Habitations & their Snares should be swept away; & your Orders (as they always ought to be) were carried out immediately. Since that Time we live happily, & we enjoy the Beneficence of the said Good Man Franklin without fear.

One Thing alone remains for us to wish in order to assure the Permanence of our Good Fortune; permit us to say it,

Bizz izzzz ouizz a ouizzzz izzzzzzzz, &c.

It is to see the two of you henceforth forming a single Household.

1784

POLITICAL
WRITINGS
AND
SATIRES

ON THE PROVIDENCE OF GOD IN THE GOVERMENT OF THE WORLD

When I consider my own Weakness, and the discerning Judgment of those who are to be my Audience, I cannot help blaming my self considerably, for this rash Undertaking of mine, it being a Thing I am altogether ill practis'd in and very much unqualified for; I am especially discouraged when I reflect that you are all my intimate Pot Companions who have heard me say a 1000 silly Things in Conversations, and therefore have not that laudable Partiality and Veneration for whatever I shall deliver that Good People commonly have for their Spiritual Guides; that You have no Reverence for my Habit, nor for the Sanctity of my Countenance; that you do not believe me inspir'd or divinely assisted, and therefore will think your Selves at Liberty to assent or dissent, approve or disapprove, of any Thing I advance, canvassing and sifting it as the private Opinion of one of your Acquaintance. These are great Disadvantages and Discouragements but I am enter'd and must proceed, humbly requesting your Patience and Attention.

I propose at this Time to discourse on the Subject of our last Conversation: the Providence of God in the Government of the World. I shall not attempt to amuse you with Flourishes of Rhetorick, were I master of that deceitful Science because I know ye are Men of substantial Reason and can easily discern between sound Argument and the false Glosses of Oratory; nor shall I endeavour to impose on your Ears, by a musical

Accent in delivery, in the Tone of one violently affected with what he says; for well I know that ye are far from being superstitious or fond of unmeaning Noise, and that ye believe a Thing to be no more true for being sung than said. I intend to offer you nothing but plain Reasoning, devoid of Art and Ornament; unsupported by the Authority of any Books or Men how sacred soever; because I know that no Authority is more convincing to Men of Reason than the Authority of Reason itself. It might be judg'd an Affront to your Understandings should I go about to prove this first Principle, the Existence of a Deity and that he is the Creator of the Universe, for that would suppose you ignorant of what all Mankind in all Ages have agreed in. I shall therefore proceed to observe:

1. That he must be a Being of great Wisdom; 2. That he must be a Being of great Goodness and 3. That he must be a Being of great Power. That he must be a Being of infinite Wisdom, appears in his admirable Order and Disposition of Things, whether we consider the heavenly Bodies, the Stars and Planets, and their wonderful regular Motions, or this Earth compounded of such an Excellent mixture of all the Elements; or the admirable Structure of Animal Bodies of such infinite Variety, and yet every one adapted to its Nature, and the Way of Life it is to be placed in, whether on Earth, in the Air or in the Waters, and so exactly that the highest and most exquisite human Reason, cannot find a fault and say this would have been better so or in another Manner, which whoever considers attentively and thoroughly will be astonish'd and swallow'd up in Admiration.

2. That the Deity is a Being of great Goodness, appears in his giving Life to so many Creatures, each of which acknowledge it a Benefit by

their Unwillingness to leave it; in his providing plentiful Sustenance for them all, and making those Things that are most useful, most common and easy to be had; such as Water necessary for almost every Creature's Drink; Air without which few could subsist, the inexpressible Benefits of Light and Sunshine to almost all Animals in general; and to Men the most useful Vegetables, such as Corn, the most useful of Metals as Iron, and the most useful Animals, as Horses, Oxen and Sheep, he has made easiest to raise, or procure in Quantity or Numbers: each of which particulars if considered seriously and carefully would fill us with the highest Love and Affection. 3. That he is a Being of infinite Power appears, in his being able to form and compound such Vast Masses of Matter as this Earth and the Sun and innumerable Planets and Stars, and give them such prodigious Motion, and yet so to govern them in their greatest Velocity as that they shall not flie off out of their appointed Bounds nor dash one against another, to their mutual Destruction; but 'tis easy to conceive his Power, when we are convinc'd of his infinite Knowledge and Wisdom; for if weak and foolish Creatures as we are, by knowing the Nature of a few Things can produce such wonderful Effects; such as for instance by knowing the Nature only of Nitre and Sea Salt mix'd we can make a Water which will dissolve the hardest Iron and by adding one Ingredient more, can make another Water which will dissolve Gold and render the most Solid Bodies fluid—and by knowing the Nature of Salt Peter Sulphur and Charcoal those mean Ingredients mix'd we can shake the Air in the most terrible Manner, destroy Ships Houses and Men at a Distance and in an Instant, overthrow Cities, rend Rocks into a Thousand Pieces, and level the highest Mountains. What Power must he possess who not only knows the Nature of every Thing in the Universe, but can make Things of new Natures with the greatest Ease and at his Pleasure!

Agreeing then that the World was at first made by a Being of infinite Wisdom, Goodness and Power, which Being we call God; The State of Things ever since and at this Time must be in one of these four following manners, viz.

1. Either he unchangeably decreed and appointed every Thing that comes to pass; and left nothing to the Course of Nature, nor allow'd any Creature free agency; or

2. Without decreeing any thing, he left all to general Nature and the Events of Free Agency in his Creatures, which he never alters or interrupts; or

3. He decreed some Things unchangeably, and left others to general Nature and the Events of Free agency, which also he never alters or interrupts; or

4. He sometimes interferes by his particular Providence and sets aside the Effects which would otherwise have been produced by any of the Above Causes.

I shall endeavour to shew the first 3 Suppositions to be inconsistent with the common Light of Reason; and that the 4th is most agreeable to it, and therefore most probably true.

In the 1. place. If you say he has in the Beginning unchangeably decreed all Things and left Nothing to Nature or free Agency. These Strange Conclusions will necessarily follow; 1. That he is now no more a God. 'Tis true indeed, before he had made such unchangeable Decree, he was a Being of Power, Almighty; but now having determin'd every

Thing, he has divested himself of all further Power, he has done and has no more to do, he has ty'd up his Hands, and has now no greater Power than an Idol of Wood or Stone; nor can there be any more Reason for praying to him or worshipping of him, than of such an Idol for the Worshippers can be never the better for such Worship. Then 2. he has decreed some things contrary to the very Notion of a wise and good Being; Such as that some of his Creatures or Children shall do all Manner of Injury to others and bring every kind of Evil upon them without Cause; that some of them shall even blaspheme him their Creator in the most horrible manner; and, which is still more highly absurd that he has decreed the greatest Part of Mankind, shall in all Ages, put up their earnest Prayers to him both in private and publickly in great Assemblies, when all the while he had so determin'd their Fate that he could not possibly grant them any Benefits on that Account, nor could such Prayers be any way available. Why then should he ordain them to make such Prayers? It cannot be imagined they are of any Service to him. Surely it is not more difficult to believe the World was made by a God of Wood or Stone, than that the God who made the World should be such a God as this.

In the 2. Place. If you say he has decreed nothing but left all things to general Nature, and the Events of Free Agency, which he never alters or interrupts. Then these Conclusions will follow; He must either utterly hide him self from the Works of his Hands, and take no Notice at all of their Proceedings natural or moral; or he must be as undoubtedly he is, a Spectator of every thing; for there can be no Reason or Ground to suppose the first—I say there can be no Reason to imagine he would make so glorious a Universe meerly to abandon it. In this Case imagine the

Deity looking on and beholding the Ways of his Creatures; some Hero's in Virtue he sees are incessantly indeavouring the Good of others, they labour thro vast difficulties, they suffer incredible Hardships and Miseries to accomplish this End, in hopes to please a Good God, and obtain his Favour, which they earnestly Pray for; what Answer can he make them within himself but this; *take the Reward Chance may give you, I do not intermeddle in these Affairs*; he sees others continually doing all manner of Evil, and bringing by their Actions Misery and Destruction among Mankind: What can he say here but this, *if Chance rewards you I shall not punish you, I am not to be concerned.* He sees the just, the innocent and the Beneficent in the Hands of the wicked and violent Oppressor; and when the good are at the Brink of Destruction they pray to him, *thou, O God, art mighty and powerful to save; help us we beseech thee*: He answers, *I cannot help you, 'tis none of my Business nor do I at all regard these things.* How is it possible to believe a wise and an infinitely Good Being can be delighted in this Circumstance; and be utterly unconcern'd what becomes of the Beings and Things he has created; for thus, we must believe him idle and unactive, and that his glorious Attributes of Power, Wisdom and Goodness are no more to be made use of.

In the Third Place. If you say he has decreed some things and left others to the Events of Nature and Free Agency, Which he never alters or interrupts; Still you unGod him, if I may be allow'd the Expression; he has nothing to do; he can cause us neither Good nor Harm; he is no more to be regarded than a lifeless Image, than Dagon, or Baall, or Bell and the Dragon; and as in both the other Suppositions foregoing, that Being which from its Power is most able to Act, from its Wisdom knows best how to act, and from its Goodness would always certainly act best, is in this Opinion supposed to become the most unactive of all Beings and remain everlastingly Idle; an Absurdity, which when considered or but barely seen, cannot be swallowed without doing the greatest Violence to common Reason, and all the Faculties of the Understanding.

We are then necessarily driven into the fourth Supposition, That the Deity sometimes interferes by his particular Providence, and sets aside the Events which would otherwise have been produc'd in the Course of Nature, or by the Free Agency of Men; and this is perfectly agreeable with what we can know of his Attributes and Perfections: But as some may doubt whether 'tis possible there should be such a Thing as free Agency in Creatures; I shall just offer one Short Argument on that Account and proceed to shew how the Duties of Religion necessary follow the Belief of a Providence. You acknowledge that God is infinitely Powerful, Wise and Good, and also a free Agent; and you will not deny that he has communicated to us part of his Wisdom, Power and Goodness; i.e. he has made us in some Degree Wise, potent and good; and is it then impossible for him to communicate any Part of his Freedom, and make us also in some Degree Free? Is not even his *infinite* Power sufficient for this? I should be glad to hear what Reason any Man can give for thinking in that Manner; 'tis sufficient for me to shew 'tis not impossible, and no Man I think can shew 'tis improbable, but much more might be offer'd to demonstrate clearly that Men are in some Degree free Agents, and accountable for their Actions; however, this I may possibly reserve for another separate Discourse hereafter if I find Occasion.

Lastly If God does not sometimes interfere by his Providence 'tis either because he cannot, or because he will not; which of these Positions will you chuse? There is a righteous Nation grievously oppress'd by a cruel Tyrant, they earnestly intreat God to deliver them; If you say he cannot, you deny his infinite Power, which you at first acknowledg'd; if you say he will not, you must directly deny his infinite Goodness. You are then of necessity oblig'd to allow, that 'tis highly reasonable to believe a Providence because tis highly absurd to believe otherwise.

Now if tis unreasonable to suppose it out of the Power of the Deity to help and favour us particularly or that we are out of his Hearing or Notice or that Good Actions do not procure more of his Favour than ill Ones. Then I conclude, that believing a Providence we have the Foundation of all true Religion; for we should love and revere that Deity for his Goodness and thank him for his Benefits; we should adore him for his Wisdom, fear him for his Power, and pray to him for his Favour and Protection; and this Religion will be a Powerful Regulater of our Actions, give us Peace and Tranquility within our own Minds, and render us Benevolent, Useful and Beneficial to others.

1730

ON TRANSPORTED FELONS

From *Virginia* we hear, that six Convicts, who were transported for fourteen Years, and shipp'd at *Liverpool*, rose at Sea, shot the Captain, overcame and confin'd the Seamen, and kept Possession of the Vessel 19 Days; that coming in Sight of *Cape Hatteras*, they hoisted out the Boat to go on shore; when a Vessel passing by, a Boy they had not confin'd, hail'd her, and attempted to tell their Condition, but was prevented; and then the Villains drove a Spike up thro' his under and upper Jaws, and wound Spunyarn round the End that came out near his Nose, to prevent his getting it out: They then cut away the Sails from the Yards, left the Ship, and went ashore. But a *New-England* Sloop coming by soon after, and seeing a Ship driving in the Sea in that Manner, boarded her, found Things as above mentioned, and carried her into *North-Carolina;* from whence a Hue and Cry went after the Villains, who had stroll'd along to *Virginia*; they were taken at *Norfolk*, and one of them confess'd the Fact; upon which they were order'd up, about two Weeks since, to *Williamsburgh*, for Trial as Pyrates.

From *Maryland* we hear, that a Convict Servant, about three Weeks since, went into his Master's House, with an Ax in his Hand, determin'd to kill his Mistress; but changing his Purpose on seeing, as he expressed it, *how d——d innocent she look'd*, he laid his Left-hand on a Block, cut it off, and threw it at her, saying, *Now make me work, if you can.*

N.B. *'Tis said this desperate Villain is now begging in*
Pennsylvania, *and 'tis thought has been seen in this City; he*

pretends to have lost his Hand by an Accident: The Publick are therefore caution'd to beware of him.

From *Bucks* County we hear, that a Convict Servant, one *John Mc-Caulefd*, imported here last Fall, has broke open and robb'd several Houses, of Goods to a considerable Value; but being apprehended at a Ferry, is committed to Prison.

Yesterday the Trial of *Samuel Saunders*, for the Murder of *Simon Girtie*, came on at the Supream Court, when the Jury return'd their Verdict *Manslaughter.*

"When we see our Papers fill'd continually with Accounts of the most audacious Robberies, the most cruel Murders, and infinite other Villainies perpetrated by Convicts transported from *Europe*, what melancholly, what terrible Reflections must it occasion! What will become of our Posterity!— These are some of thy Favours, BRITAIN! Thou art called our MOTHER COUNTRY; but what good *Mother* ever sent *Thieves* and *Villains* to accompany her *Children;* to corrupt some with their infectious Vices, and murder the rest? What *Father* ever endeavour'd to spread the *Plague* in his Family!—We do not ask Fish, but thou givest us *Serpents*, and worse than Serpents!—In what can *Britain* show a more Sovereign Contempt for us, than by emptying their *Jails* into our Settlements; unless they would likewise empty their *Jakes* on our Tables?—What must we think of that B——d, which has advis'd the Repeal of every Law we have hitherto made to prevent this Deluge of Wickedness overwhelming us; and with this *cruel* Sarcasm, *That these Laws were against the* Publick Utility, *for they tended to prevent the* IMPROVEMENT *and* WELL-PEOPLING *of the Colonies!* —And what must we think of those Merchants, who for the sake of a little paltry Gain, will be concern'd in importing and disposing of these abominable Cargoes?"

The Pennsylvania Gazette, APRIL 11, 1751

RATTLE-SNAKES FOR FELONS

To the Printers of the Gazette.

By a Passage in one of your late Papers, I understand that the Government at home will not suffer our mistaken Assemblies to make any Law for preventing or discouraging the Importation of Convicts from Great Britain, for this kind Reason, '*That such Laws are against the Publick Utility, as they tend to prevent the* IMPROVEMENT *and* WELL PEOPLING *of the Colonies.*'

Such a tender *parental* Concern in our *Mother Country* for the *Welfare* of her Children, calls aloud for the highest *Returns* of Gratitude and Duty. This every one must be sensible of: But 'tis said, that in our present Circumstances it is absolutely impossible for us to make *such* as are adequate to the Favour. I own it; but nevertheless let us do our Endeavour. 'Tis something to show a grateful Disposition.

In some of the uninhabited Parts of these Provinces, there are Numbers of these venomous Reptiles we call RATTLE-SNAKES; Felons-convict from the Beginning of the World: These, whenever we meet with them, we put to Death, by Virtue of an old Law, *Thou shalt bruise his Head*. But as this is a sanguinary Law, and may seem too cruel; and as however mischievous those Creatures are with us, they may possibly change their Natures, if they were to change the Climate; I would humbly propose, that this general Sentence of *Death* be changed for *Transportation*.

In the Spring of the Year, when they first creep out of their Holes, they are feeble, heavy, slow, and easily taken; and if a small Bounty were allow'd *per* Head, some Thousands might be collected annually, and *transported* to Britain. There I would propose to have them carefully distributed in *St. James's Park*, in the *Spring-Gardens* and other Places of Pleasure about *London*; in the Gardens of all the Nobility and Gentry throughout the Nation; but particularly in the Gardens of the *Prime Ministers*, the *Lords of Trade* and *Members of Parliament*; for to them we are *most particularly* obliged.

There is no human Scheme so perfect, but some Inconveniencies may be objected to it: Yet when the Conveniencies far exceed, the Scheme is judg'd rational, and fit to be executed. Thus Inconveniencies have been objected to that *good* and *wise* Act of Parliament, by virtue of which all the *Newgates* and *Dungeons* in *Britain* are emptied into the Colonies. It has been said, that these Thieves and Villains introduc'd among us, spoil the Morals of Youth in the Neighbourhoods that entertain them, and perpetrate many horrid Crimes: But let not *private Interests* obstruct *publick Utility*. Our *Mother* knows what is best for us. What is a little *Housebreaking, Shoplifting,* or *Highway Robbing*; what is a *Son* now and then *corrupted* and *hang'd*, a Daughter *debauch'd* and *pox'd*, a Wife *stabb'd*, a Husband's *Throat cut*, or a Child's *Brains beat out* with an Axe, compar'd with this 'IMPROVEMENT and WELL PEOPLING of the Colonies!'

Thus it may perhaps be objected to my Scheme, that the *Rattle-Snake* is a mischievous Creature, and that his changing his Nature with the Clime is a mere Supposition, not yet confirm'd by sufficient Facts. What then? Is not Example more prevalent than Precept? And may not the honest rough British Gentry, by a Familiarity with these Reptiles, learn to *creep*, and to insinuate, and to *slaver*, and to *wriggle* into Place (and perhaps to *poison* such as stand in their Way) Qualities of no small Advantage to Courtiers! In comparison of which '*Improvement* and *Publick Utility*,' what is a *Child* now and then kill'd by their venomous Bite,— or even a favourite *Lap-Dog*?

I would only add, That this Exporting of Felons to the Colonies, may be consider'd as a *Trade*, as well as in the Light of a *Favour*. Now all Commerce implies *Returns*: Justice requires them: There can be no Trade without them. And *Rattle-Snakes* seem the most *suitable Returns* for the *Human Serpents* sent by our *Mother* Country. In this, however, as in every other Branch of Trade, she will have the Advantage of us. She will reap *equal* Benefits without equal Risque of the Inconveniencies and Dangers. For the *Rattle-Snake* gives Warning before he attempts his Mischief; which the Convict does not. I am

Yours, &c.

Americanus.

The Pennsylvania Gazette, MAY 9, 1751

HUMOUROUS REASONS FOR RESTORING CANADA

Mr. Chronicle,

We Britons are a nation of statesmen and politicians; we are privy councellors by birthright; and therefore take it much amiss when we are told by some of your correspondents, 'that it is not proper to expose to public view the many good reasons there are for restoring Canada,' (*if we reduce it.*)

I have, with great industry, been able to procure a full account of those reasons, and shall make no secret of them among ourselves. Here they are. —Give them to all your readers; that is, to all that can read, in the King's dominions.

1. We should restore Canada; because an uninterrupted trade with the Indians throughout a vast country, where the communication by water is so easy, would encrease our commerce, *already too great*, and occasion a large additional demand for our manufactures,* *already too dear.*

2. We should restore it, lest, thro' a greater plenty of beaver, broad-brimmed hats become cheaper to that unmannerly sect, the Quakers.

---

*Every Indian now wears a woollen blanket, a linnen shirt, and cloth stockings; besides a knife, a hatchet and a gun; and they use a variety of other European and Indian goods, which they pay for in skins and furs.

3. We should restore Canada, that we may *soon* have a new war, and another opportunity of spending two or three millions a year in America; there being great danger of our growing too rich, our European expences not being sufficient to drain our immense treasures.

4. We should restore it, that we may have occasion constantly to employ, in time of war, a fleet and army in those parts; for otherwise we might be too strong at home.

5. We should restore it, that the French may, by means of their Indians, carry on, (as they have done for these 100 years past even in times of peace between the two crowns) a constant scalping war against our colonies, and thereby stint their growth; for, otherwise, the children might in time be as tall as their mother.*

6. What tho' the blood of thousands of unarmed English farmers, surprized and assassinated in their fields; of harmless women and children murdered in their beds; doth at length call for vengeance;—what tho' the Canadian measure of iniquity be full, and if ever any country did, that country now certainly does, deserve the judgment of *extirpation*;—yet let not us be the executioners of Divine justice;—it will look as if Englishmen were revengeful.

7. Our colonies, 'tis true, have exerted themselves beyond their strength, on the expectations we gave them of driving the French from Canada; but tho' we ought to keep faith with our Allies, it is not necessary with our children. That might teach them (against Scripture) to *put their trust in Princes*: Let 'em learn to trust in God.

---

* This reason is seriously given by who do not wish well to the Colonies: But, is it not too like the Egyptain Politics practised by Pharoah, destroying the young males to prevent the increase of the children of Isreal?

8.   Should we not restore Canada, it would look as if our statesmen had *courage* as well as our soldiers; but what have statesmen to do with *courage?* Their proper character is *wisdom.*

9.   What can be *braver,* than to show all Europe we can afford to lavish our best blood as well as our treasure, in conquests we do not intend to keep? Have we not plenty of *Howe's,* and *Wolfe's,* &c. &c. &c. in every regiment?

10.   The French* have long since openly declar'd, *'que les Anglois & les François sont incompatible dans cette partie de l'Amerique;'* 'that our people and theirs were incompatible in that part of the continent of America:' *'que rien n'etoit plus important à l'etat, que de delivrer leur colonie du facheux voisinage des Anglois;'* 'that nothing was of more importance to France, than delivering its colony from the troublesome neighbourhood of the English;' to which end, there was an avowed project on foot *'pour chasser premierement les Anglois de la Nouvelle York;'* 'to drive the English in the first place out of the province of New York;' *'& apres la prise de la capitale, il falloit* (says the scheme) *la* BRULER & RUINER *le pays jusqu' a Orange;'* 'and after taking the capital, to *burn it,* and *ruin* (that is, *make a desart* of) the whole country, quite up to Albany.' Now, if we do not fairly leave the French in Canada, till they have a favourable opportunity of putting their *burning* and *ruining* schemes in execution, will it not look as if we were afraid of them?

11.   Their historian, Charlevoix, in his IVth book, also tells us, that when Canada was formerly taken by the English, it was a question at

---

* Histoire Generale de la Novuvelle France, par Charle voix. Liv. xii.

the court of France, whether they should endeavour to recover it; for, says he, '*bien de gens douterent si l'on avoit fait une veritable perte;*' 'many thought it was not really a loss.' But tho' various reasons were given why it was scarce worth recovering, '*le seul motive* (says he) *d'empecher les Anglois de se rendre trop puissans—étoit plus que suffissant pour nous engager a recouvrer Quebec, a quelque prix que ce fût;*' 'the single motive of preventing the increase of *English* power, was more than sufficient to engage us in recovering Quebec, *what price soever it might cost us.*' Here we see the high value they put on that country, and the reason of their valuing it so highly. Let us then, *oblige them* in this (to them) so important an article, and be assured they will *never prove ungrateful.*

I will not dissemble, Mr. *Chronicle*; that in answer to all these reasons and motives for restoring Canada, I have heard one that appears to have some weight on the other side of the question. It is said, that nations, as well as private persons, should, for their honour's sake, take care to preserve a *consistence of character*: that it has always been the character of the English to fight strongly, and negotiate weakly; generally agreeing to restore, at a peace, what they ought to have kept, and to keep what they had better have restored: then, if it would really, according to the preceding reasons, be prudent and right to restore Canada, we ought, say these objectors, to keep it; otherwise *we shall be inconsistent with ourselves.* I shall not take upon myself to weigh these different reasons, but offer the whole to the consideration of the public. Only permit me to suggest, that there is one method of avoiding fairly all future dispute about the propriety of *keeping* or *restoring* Canada; and that is, *let us never take it.* The French still hold out at Montreal and Trois Rivieres, in hopes of succour from France. Let us be but *a little too late* with our ships in the river St. Laurence, so that the enemy may get their supplies up next spring, as they did the last, with reinforcements sufficient to enable them to recover Quebec, and there is an end of the question. I am, Sir, Yours, &c.

A. Z.

The London Chronicle, DECEMBER 27, 1759

PAX QUÆRITUR BELLO

To the Printer of the Public Advertiser.
Pax quæritur Bello.

SIR,

The very important Controversy being next Tuesday to be finally determined between the Mother Country and their rebellious American Children, I shall think myself happy if I can furnish any Hints that may be of public Utility.

There are some Persons besides the Americans so amazingly stupid, as to distinguish in this Dispute between *Power* and *Right*, as tho' the former did not always imply the latter. The Right of Conquest invests the Conqueror with Authority to establish what Laws he pleases, however contrary to the Laws of Nature, and the common Rights of Mankind.

Examine every Form of Government at this Day subsisting on the Face of the Globe, from the absolute Despotism of the Grand Sultan to the Democratic Government of the City of Geneva, and it will be found that the Exertion of Power in those Hands with whom it is lodged, however unconstitutional, is always justified. The Reign of the *Stuarts* might serve to exemplify this Observation. Happy it was for the Nation that, upon Trial, the superior Power was found to be in the People. The American Plea of *Right*, their Appeal to Magna Charta, must of course be set aside; and I make no Doubt but the Grand Council of the Nation will at all Hazards insist upon an absolute Submission to the Tax imposed upon them. But that they will comply without coercive Measures, is to me a Matter of very great Doubt: For when we consider, that these People, especially the more Northern Colonies, are the Descendants of your Pymms, Hampdens, and others of the like Stamp, those outrageous Assertors of Civil and Religious Liberties; that they have been nursed up in the same Old English Principles; that a little more than a Century ago their Forefathers, many of them of Family and Fortune, left their native Land, and endured all the Distresses and Hardships which are the necessary Consequences of an Establishment in a new uncultivated Country, surrounded with a cruel Blood-thirsty Enemy, oftentimes severely pinched with Cold and Hunger; and all this to enjoy unmolested that Liberty which they thought was infringed: I say, however these People may be mistaken, they will not tamely give up what they call their natural, their constitutional Rights. Force must therefore be made use of.

Now in order to bring these People to a proper Temper, I have a Plan to propose, which I think cannot fail, and which will be entirely consistent with the Oeconomy at present so much in Vogue. It is so cheap a Way of going to work, that even Mr. G—— G——, that great Oeconomist, could have no reasonable Objection to it.

Let Directions be given, that Two Thousand Highlanders be immediately raised, under proper Officers of their own. It ought to be no Objection, that they were in the Rebellion in Forty-five: If Roman Catholics, the better. The C——l at present in the P——ze Service may be at their Head. Transport them early in the Spring to Quebec: There with the Canadians, natural Enemies to our Colonists, who would voluntarily engage, might make a Body of Five or Six Thousand Men; and I doubt not, by artful Management, and the Value of two or three Thousand Pounds in Presents, with the Hopes of Plunder, as likewise a Gratuity for every Scalp, the Savages on the Frontiers might be engaged to join, at least they would make a Diversion, which could not fail of being useful. I could point out a very proper General to command the Expedition; he is of a very sanguine Disposition, and has an inordinate Thirst for Fame, and besides has the Hearts of the Canadians. He might march from Canada, cross the Lakes, and fall upon these People without their expecting or being prepared for him, and with very little Difficulty overrun the whole Country.

The Business might be done without employing any of the Regular Troops quartered in the Country, and I think it would be best they should remain neuter, as it is to be feared they would be rather backward in embruing their Hands in the Blood of their Brethren and Fellow Subjects.

I would propose, that all the Capitals of the several Provinces should be burnt to the Ground, and that they cut the Throats of all the

Inhabitants, Men, Women, and Children, and scalp them, to serve as an Example; that all the Shipping should be destroyed, which will effectually prevent Smuggling, and save the Expence of Guarda Costas.

No Man in his Wits, after such terrible Military Execution, will refuse to purchase stamp'd Paper. If any one should hesitate, five or six Hundred Lashes in a cold frosty Morning would soon bring him to Reason.

If the Massacre should be objected to, as it would too much depopulate the Country, it may be replied, that the Interruption this Method would occasion to Commerce, would cause so many Bankruptcies, such Numbers of Manufacturers and Labourers would be unemployed, that, together with the Felons from our Gaols, we should soon be enabled to transport such Numbers to repeople the Colonies, as to make up for any Deficiency which Example made it necessary to sacrifice for the Public Good. Great Britain might then reign over a loyal and submissive People, and be morally certain, that no Act of Parliament would ever after be disputed.

Your's,

Pacificus.

Jan. 23, 1766

The Public Advertiser, January 26, 1766

ON CIVIL WAR

To the Printer of the Public Advertiser.

Sir,

Threescore Years did the oppressed United Provinces maintain a War in Defence of their Liberties against the then powerful Kingdom of *Spain*, with all the Wealth of the *Indies* at it's Command; and finally obliged it to acknowledge their Independency in a formal Treaty, sitting down with the Loss of Territory, Treasure and Reputation, and with a broken Strength that has never since been recovered.

Contractors, jobbing mercantile Members of Parliament, Officers starving on Half Pay, and Gunsmiths who *toast*, as the Papers tell us, *a speedy and a perpetual War*, may wish, rather than no War at all, for a *Civil* one in America. These in all Conversations, to encourage us in undertaking it, slight the Strength of those distant People, think nothing of that Enthusiasm for Liberty, which in other Countries and Ages has supplied all Deficiencies, and enabled a weak People to battle the Efforts of a stronger; but tell us that half a dozen Regiments are sufficient to reduce in less than a Year every Province on the Continent. Half a dozen being once engaged in this blessed Service, it is easy to write and shew the Necessity for more: The more there are, the greater the Profits to those Gentry. And whatever becomes of us poor Devils that live by Manufactures or by Trade, that are to pay Taxes, or that have Money in the Funds, *they* will amass Fortunes, buy our Estates, bribe our Boroughs, and vote in Parliament the Rectitude of the Measure.

I believe our Officers and Soldiers as brave as any in the World; and from that very Opinion of their Bravery I conjecture they would not generally relish the being ordered on this murdering Service against their Countrymen; to shed English Blood, to stifle the British Spirit of Liberty now rising in the Colonies; that LIBERTY which we should rather wish to see nourished and preserved there, as on a loss of it here (which from our vices is perhaps not far distant) we or our Posterity may have Occasion to resort to and participate of; and possibly some of the ablest Officers may chuse, with Sir *Jeffery Amherst*, rather to resign their Commissions. But whatever may be the Bravery and military Prowess of our Troops, and whatever the Zeal with which they would proceed in such a War, there are Reasons that make me suspect it will not be so soon terminated as some Folks would have us believe.

My reasons are drawn chiefly from a Computation founded on *Facts*. It is well known that America is a Country full of Forests, Mountains, &c. That in such a Country a small irregular Force can give Abundance of Trouble to a regular one that is much greater: And that, in the last War, *one* of the fifteen Colonies we now have there (and one far short of being the strongest) held out *five Years* against *twenty-five thousand* British regular Troops, joined by *twenty-five thousand* Colonists on their own Pay, and aided by a strong Fleet of Men of War. What the Expence was to this Nation, our Treasury Books and augmented Debt may shew. The Expence to America, as their Pay was higher, could not be much less. The Colony we made War upon was indeed aided by *France*, but during the whole Contest not with more than five thousand Men. Now supposing that the twenty-five thousand Colonists that then joined us should hereafter be against us, and that this makes no Difference, and considering that instead of *one* Colony to conquer, we are to have *fifteen*, and that possibly some of our good Neighbours may think of making a Diversion in their Favour, I apprehend it not out of the Way to allow *five* Years still to a Colony; and this, by my Computation, will amount to just *seventy-five* Years. I hope Messieurs the Company of Gunsmiths will for the present be so good as to be content with a Civil War of *seventy-five* Years, as perhaps we may scarce be able to afford them a *perpetual* one.

And what are we to gain by this War, by which our Trade and Manufactures are to be ruined, our Strength divided and diminished, our Debt increased, and our Reputation, as a generous Nation, and Lovers of Liberty, given up and lost? Why, we are to convert Millions of the King's loyal Subjects into Rebels, for the sake of establishing a newly-claimed power in P—— to tax a distant People, whose Abilities and Circumstances they cannot be acquainted with, who have a constitutional Power of taxing themselves; who have never refused to give us voluntarily more than we can ever expect to wrest from them by Force; and by our Trade with whom we gain Millions a Year!

And is there not *one* wise and good Man to be found in *Britain*, who can propose some conciliating Measure that may prevent this terrible Mischief?—I fear not one. For

Quos Deus vult perdere, dementat prius!

The Public Advertiser, AUGUST 25, 1768

THE RISE AND PRESENT STATE OF OUR MISUNDERSTANDING

To the PRINTER *of the* LONDON CHRONICLE.

SIR,

Much abuse has lately been thrown out against the Colonies, by the Writers for the American part of our Administration. Our Fellow Subjects there are continually represented as Rebels to their Sovereign, and inimical to the British nation; in order to create a dislike of them here, that the harsh measures which have been taken, and are intended against them, may not be blamed by the People of England. Therefore to prevent our being led into mistakes in so important a business, it is fit that a full and particular account of the rise and present state of our misunderstanding with the Colonies should be laid before the Public. This, from the opportunities I have had, and the pains I have taken to inform myself, I think I am enabled to do, and I hope I shall do it with truth and candor.

The fact then is, that there is not nor has been any rebellion in America. If the rescue of a seizure by Smugglers, or the drubbing an Informer or low Custom-house Officer, were rebellion, England, Scotland, and Ireland, might be said to be in rebellion almost every week in the year; and instances of that kind are much fewer in America than here. The Americans were ever attached to the House of Hanover, and honour their present gracious Sovereign sincerely. This is therefore a groundless calumny. Nor have they any enmity to Britain: they love and honour the name of Englishman; they were fond of English manners, fashions, and manufactures; they had no desire of breaking the connection between the two countries, but wished a perpetual intercourse of good offices, commerce, and friendship. They are always willing to give aids to the Crown in proportion to their abilities: They think, however, and have always thought, that they themselves have alone the right of granting their own money, by their own Representatives in Assembly met, and that the Parliament of Britain hath no right to raise a revenue from them without their consent.

The Parliament hath, nevertheless, of late made several attempts to raise such a revenue among them.

Heretofore, whenever the Colonies thought themselves aggrieved by British government, they applied for redress by humble petition; and it was usual to receive and consider their petitions, and give them a reasonable answer.

They proceeded in the same manner on the late occasions. They sent over petitions after petitions to the House of Commons, and some to the House of Lords. These were scarce any of them received. Some (offered while the acts were under consideration) were refused on this reason, that it was against an order of the House to receive petitions against money bills; others, because they contained expressions that called the right of Parliament in question; and therefore, it was said, no Member dared to present them. Finding the petitions of separate Colonies were not attended to, they thought to give them more weight by petitioning jointly. To this end a congress of Committees from all the Assemblies was held at New York, when petitions to the King and both Houses of Parliament were agreed to and sent hither. But these could not be received, or were rejected, on the pretence that the congress was an illegal assembly which had no right to petition. Lastly, on occasion of the Duty Act, the Assemblies proposed by a correspondence with each other to obtain attention, by sending at the same time similar petitions. These were intended to the King their Sovereign, requesting his gracious influence with his Parliament to procure them redress. But this they were told by the American Minister was a FLAGITIOUS* attempt! All the Governors were by him directed to prevent it, or to dissolve the Assemblies that persisted in it; and several of them were accordingly dissolved. And of those petitions that nevertheless came hither and were presented, it is said that no notice was ever taken, or any answer given to them.

By this management the ancient well contrived channel of communication between the head and members of this great Empire, thro' which the notice of grievances could be received that remedies might be applied, hath been cut off. How wisely, the Publick will judge. History of a similar conduct in the Ministry of Spain with regard to the Low Countries, makes one doubt a little the prudence (in any Government how great soever) of discouraging Petitions, and treating Petitioners (how mean soever) with contempt.

Instead of *preventing* complaints by removing the causes, it has been thought best that Soldiers should be sent to *silence* them.

The Soldiers have behaved in such a manner as to occasion more complaints.

They took possession of the publick building in which the Assembly or Parliament of New England usually convenes, obliged the

---

* See Lord Ho's Letters to the Governors.

Members to pass through lanes of men in arms to get to their Chamber, disturbing them in their debates by drumming and piping in and round the House, and pointed the cannon against the doors, treating the Province and People with every indignity and insult, proper to provoke their resentment, and produce some rash action that might justify making a massacre among them. And they have fired upon and murdered several of the inhabitants.

The Americans, upon the treatment their Petitions had repeatedly received, determined to petition no more: But said to one another, "We are too remote from Britain to have our complaints regarded by the Parliament there, especially as we have no share in their Election, nor any Representatives among them. They will not hear *us*, but perhaps they will hear *their own people*, their Merchants and Manufacturers, who are maintained and enriched in some degree by the commerce with our country. Let us agree to with-hold that commerce till our grievances are redressed. This will afford those people a foundation for petitioning, and they will be attended to as they were on a former occasion, and meet with success." This reasoning and expectation were the sole foundation of the Non-Importation agreements in America, and *not any enmity to Britain*.

In this expectation it seems they were mistaken. The Merchants trading to North America not well liking the Ministry, unwilling to solicit or be obliged to them for any thing, and hoping soon to see a change for others more to their mind, were backward in petitioning the Parliament. And when they did petition, the City being out of favour at Court, their Petition was very little attended to, and produced no effect. To prevent the Manufacturers from taking any part in the affair, they have been

artfully amused with assurances that the Colonies could not long subsist without the trade, that manufactures among themselves were impossible, that they might depend there would be an extraordinary demand
for goods as soon as the total want of conveniencies should compel the
Americans to resume the commerce; and therefore they would do well to
be quiet, mind their business, and get a great stock of goods beforehand
to be ready for that demand, when the advanced price would make them
ample amends for the delay.

In the mean time the Merchants in America have reaped great
advantages. They have sold off most of the old goods that lay upon their
hands; they have got in most of their debts from the people, and have
in a great measure discharged their debt to England, that bore a heavy
interest; this they have done at an advantage of near 20 per cent. in most
of the Colonies, by the lowness of exchange, occasioned by the non-
importation; and this nation has lost near that proportion (if I am rightly
informed) on all the money drawn for these by British Agents, to pay and
provide for the troops and ships of war, and to discharge other expences
of contingent service. This loss must amount to a very great sum, besides
the loss in commerce.

Many of these Merchants in America, however, having nearly com-
pleated these points, and seeing the main end of their agreement, (the
total abolition of the duties) not likely to be so soon obtained as they expected, begin to grow uneasy under the delay, and are rather desirous of
altering the agreement made against general importation, and reducing
it to the exclusion of those commercial articles only, on which the duties
are, or shall be imposed. But the generality of the people in America, the

artisans in the towns, and the farmers throughout the country, finding the non-importation advantageous to them all; to the artisans, as it occasions fuller employment, and encourages the beginners that introduce new arts; and to the farmers, as it prevents much useless expence in their families, and thereby enables them more expeditiously to improve their plantations to the raising a greater produce, at the same time that it is a spur to domestic industry, in such manufactures as though not fine, are now become fashionable and reputable, and from their superior strength are much more serviceable than the flimsy fineries that used to be made for them in Britain; and all feeling the advantage of having had money returned into the country for its produce, from Spain, Portugal, Italy, (and even from England since the balance of trade has turned against her) instead of those British superfluities for which all that cash was formerly remitted, or ordered into England. I say, the generality of the people in America, pleased with this situation of things, and relishing the sweets of it, have now taken the lead, in a great degree, out of the hands of the Merchants, and in town and county meetings are entering into solemn resolutions not to purchase or consume British commodities, if they are imported, till the acts they esteem injurious to their privileges are repealed; and that if any Merchants do import before that time, they will mark them as enemies to their country, and never deal with them when the trade shall be opened. This is now become a restraint upon the Merchants. A party, however, of those at New-York, have broken through the agreement, and ordered goods; and the Merchants here, who had long lain idle, being rejoiced at this opening, have sent them over immense quantities, expecting a quick sale and speedy returns. But the event is yet very uncertain. The trade of New-York was chiefly with East New Jersey and Connecticut, their two neighbouring Colonies, and these have resolved to have no farther dealings with that city. Several counties, too, of the Province of New-York, and the greatest part of the inhabitants of the city itself, have protested against the infraction of the agreement, and determined not to buy or use the goods when they arrive. So that the exporters begin now to apprehend that their sanguine hopes will be disappointed. And as Rhode Island has returned to the agreement, some think it not unlikely that New-York may do the same.

What remedy, if any, the wisdom of Parliament shall think fit to apply to these disorders, a little time will shew. Mean while, I cannot but think that those writers, who busily employ their talents in endeavouring to exasperate this nation against the Colonies, are doing it a very ill office: For their virulent writings being dispersed among the inhabitants of the Plantations (who read all our papers and pamphlets, and imagine them of greater estimation here than they really are) do in some degree irritate the Colonists against a country which treats them, as they imagine, so injuriously:—And on our side, as nothing is likely to be well done that is done in anger; as customers are not naturally brought back to a shop by unkind usage; as the Americans are growing, and soon will be, a great people, and their friendship or enmity become daily of more and more consequence; as their fisheries, their coasting trade, their West-Indian and European trades, greatly increase the numbers of English seamen, and thereby augment our naval power; as their joint operations with our's in time of war must make the whole national effort more weighty and more effectual; as enmities between countries, fostered and promoted till they have taken root, are scarce ever to be eradicated; and, when those countries are under the same Prince, such enmities are of the most mischievous consequence, encouraging foreign enemies, weakening the whole empire, and tending to its dissolution; therefore I cannot but wish, that no steps may be taken against the Colonists, tending to abridge their privileges, alter their charters, or inflict punishments on them, at the instance of *angry Governors, discarded Agents, or rash indiscreet Officers of the Customs,* who, having quarrelled with them, are their enemies, and are daily irritating Government here against them, by misrepresentations of their actions, and aggravations of their faults, with much malice: I hope the great principle of common justice, that *no man should be condemned unheard,* will not by us be violated in the case of a whole people; and that lenient measures will be adopted, as most likely to heal the wound effectually: For harsh treatment may increase the inflammation, make the cure less practicable, and in time bring on the necessity of an amputation; death indeed to the severed limb, weakness and lameness to the mutilated body.

The London Chronicle, NOVEMBER 8, 1770

RULES BY WHICH A GREAT EMPIRE MAY BE REDUCED TO A SMALL ONE

[Presented privately to a late Minister, *when he entered upon his Administration; and now first published.]*

An ancient Sage valued himself upon this, that tho' he could not fiddle, he knew how to make a *great City* of a *little one.* The Science that I, a modern Simpleton, am about to communicate is the very reverse.

I address myself to all Ministers who have the Management of extensive Dominions, which from their very Greatness are become troublesome to govern, because the Multiplicity of their Affairs leaves no Time for *fiddling.*

I.   In the first Place, Gentlemen, you are to consider, that a great Empire, like a great Cake, is most easily diminished at the Edges. Turn your Attention therefore first to your remotest Provinces; that as you get rid of them, the next may follow in Order.

II.   That the Possibility of this Separation may always exist, take special Care the Provinces are never incorporated with the Mother Country, that they do not enjoy the same common Rights, the same Privileges in Commerce, and that they are governed by severer Laws, all of *your enacting,* without allowing them any Share in the Choice of the Legislators. By carefully making and preserving such Distinctions, you will (to keep to my Simile of the Cake) act like a wise Gingerbread Baker, who, to facilitate a Division, cuts his Dough half through in those Places, where, when bak'd, he would have it *broken to Pieces.*

III. These remote Provinces have perhaps been acquired, purchas'd, or conquer'd, at the *sole Expence* of the Settlers or their Ancestors, without the Aid of the Mother Country. If this should happen to increase her *Strength* by their growing Numbers ready to join in her Wars, her *Commerce* by their growing Demand for her Manufactures, or her *Naval Power* by greater Employment for her Ships and Seamen, they may probably suppose some Merit in this, and that it entitles them to some Favour; you are therefore to *forget it all,* or resent it as if they had done you Injury. If they happen to be zealous Whigs, Friends of Liberty, nurtur'd in Revolution Principles, *remember all that* to their Prejudice, and contrive to punish it: For such Principles, after a Revolution is thoroughly established, are of *no more Use,* they are even *odious* and *abominable.*

IV. However peaceably your Colonies have submitted to your Government, shewn their Affection to your Interest, and patiently borne their Grievances, you are to *suppose* them always inclined to revolt, and treat them accordingly. Quarter Troops among them, who by their Insolence may *provoke* the rising of Mobs, and by their Bullets and Bayonets *suppress* them. By this Means, like the Husband who uses his Wife ill *from Suspicion,* you may in Time convert your *Suspicions* into *Realities.*

V. Remote Provinces must have *Governors,* and *Judges,* to represent the Royal Person, and execute every where the delegated Parts of his Office and Authority. You Ministers know, that much of the Strength of Government depends on the *Opinion* of the People; and much of that Opinion on the Choice of Rulers placed immediately over them. If you send them wise and good Men for Governors, who study the Interest of the Colonists, and advance their Prosperity, they will think their King wise and good, and that he wishes the Welfare of his Subjects. If you send them learned and upright Men for Judges, they will think him a Lover of Justice. This may attach your Provinces more to his Government. You are therefore to be careful who you recommend for those Offices.—If you can find Prodigals who have ruined their Fortunes, broken Gamesters or Stock-Jobbers, these may do well as *Governors*; for they will probably be rapacious, and provoke the People by their Extortions. Wrangling Proctors and petty-fogging Lawyers too are not amiss, for they will be for ever disputing and quarrelling with their little Parliaments. If withal they should be ignorant, wrong-headed and insolent, so much the better. Attorneys Clerks and Newgate Solicitors will do for *Chief-Justices*, especially if they hold their Places *during your Pleasure*:—And all will contribute to impress those ideas of your Government that are proper for a People *you would wish to renounce it.*

VI. To confirm these Impressions, and strike them deeper, whenever the Injured come to the Capital with Complaints of Mal-administration, Oppression, or Injustice, punish such Suitors with long Delay, enormous Expence, and a final Judgment in Favour of the Oppressor. This will have an admirable Effect every Way. The Trouble of future Complaints will be prevented, and Governors and Judges will be encouraged to farther Acts of Oppression and Injustice; and thence the People may become more disaffected, *and at length desperate.*

VII. When such Governors have crammed their Coffers, and made themselves so odious to the People that they can no longer remain among them with Safety to their Persons, recall and *reward* them with Pensions. You may make them *Baronets* too, if that respectable Order should not think fit to resent it. All will contribute to encourage new Governors in the same Practices, and make the supreme Government *detestable.*

VIII. If when you are engaged in War, your Colonies should vie in liberal Aids of Men and Money against the common Enemy, upon your simple Requisition, and give far beyond their Abilities, reflect, that a Penny taken from them by your Power is more honourable to you than a Pound presented by their Benevolence. Despise therefore their voluntary Grants, and resolve to harrass them with novel Taxes. They will probably complain to your Parliaments that they are taxed by a Body in which they have no Representative, and that this is contrary to common Right. They will petition for Redress. Let the Parliaments flout their Claims, reject their Petitions, refuse even to suffer the reading of them, and treat the Petitioners with the utmost Contempt. Nothing can have a better Effect, in producing the Alienation proposed; for though many can forgive Injuries, *none ever forgave Contempt.*

IX. In laying these Taxes, never regard the heavy Burthens those remote People already undergo, in defending their own Frontiers, supporting their own provincial Governments, making new Roads, building Bridges, Churches and other public Edifices, which in old Countries have been done to your Hands by your Ancestors, but which occasion constant Calls and Demands on the Purses of a new People. Forget the *Restraints* you lay on their Trade for *your own* Benefit, and the Advantage a *Monopoly* of this Trade gives your exacting Merchants. Think nothing of the Wealth those Merchants and your Manufacturers acquire by the Colony Commerce; their encreased Ability thereby to pay Taxes at home; their accumulating, in the Price of their Commodities, most of those Taxes, and so levying them from their consuming Customers: All this, and the Employment and Support of Thousands of your Poor by the Colonists, you are *intirely to forget*. But remember to make your arbitrary Tax more grievous to your Provinces, by public Declarations importing that your Power of taxing them has *no Limits*, so that when you take from them without their Consent a Shilling in the Pound, you have a clear Right to the other nineteen. This will probably weaken every Idea of *Security in their Property*, and convince them that under such a Government *they have nothing they can call their own*; which can scarce fail of producing the *happiest Consequences*!

X. Possibly indeed some of them might still comfort themselves, and say, 'Though we have no Property, we have yet *something* left that is valuable; we have constitutional *Liberty* both of Person and of Conscience. This King, these Lords, and these Commons, who it seems are too remote from us to know us and feel for us, cannot take from us our *Habeas Corpus* Right, or our Right of Trial *by a Jury of our Neighbours*: They cannot deprive us of the Exercise of our Religion, alter our ecclesiastical Constitutions, and compel us to be Papists if they please, or Mahometans.' To annihilate this Comfort, begin by Laws to perplex their Commerce with infinite Regulations impossible to be remembered and observed; ordain Seizures of their Property for every Failure; take away the Trial of such Property by Jury, and give it to arbitrary Judges of your own appointing, and of the lowest Characters in the Country, whose Salaries and Emoluments are to arise out of the Duties or Condemnations, and whose Appointments are *during Pleasure*. Then let there be a formal Declaration of both Houses, that Opposition to your Edicts is *Treason*, and that Persons suspected of Treason in the Provinces may, according to some obsolete Law, be seized and sent to the Metropolis of the Empire for Trial; and pass an Act that those there charged with certain other Offences shall be sent away in Chains from their Friends and Country to be tried in the same Manner for Felony. Then erect a new Court of Inquisition among them, accompanied by an armed Force, with Instructions to transport all such suspected Persons, to be ruined by the Expence if they bring over Evidences to prove their Innocence, or be found guilty and hanged if they can't afford it. And lest the People should think you cannot possibly go any farther, pass another solemn declaratory Act, that 'King, Lords, and Commons had, hath, and of Right ought to have, full Power and Authority to make Statutes of sufficient Force and Validity to bind the unrepresented Provinces IN ALL CASES WHATSOEVER.' This will include *spiritual* with temporal; and taken together, must operate wonderfully to your Purpose, by convincing them, that they are at present under a Power something like that spoken of in the Scriptures, which can not only *kill their Bodies*, but *damn their Souls* to all Eternity, by compelling them, if it pleases, *to worship the Devil.*

XI.   To make your Taxes more odious, and more likely to procure Resistance, send from the Capital a Board of Officers to superintend the Collection, composed of the most *indiscreet, ill-bred* and *insolent* you can find. Let these have large Salaries out of the extorted Revenue, and live in open grating Luxury upon the Sweat and Blood of the Industrious, whom they are to worry continually with groundless and expensive Prosecutions before the above-mentioned arbitrary Revenue-Judges, all *at the Cost of the Party prosecuted* tho' acquitted, because *the King is to pay no Costs.*—Let these Men *by your Order* be exempted from all the common Taxes and Burthens of the Province, though they and their Property are protected by its Laws. If any Revenue Officers are *suspected* of the least Tenderness for the People, discard them. If others are justly complained of, protect and reward them. If any of the Under-officers behave so as to provoke the People to drub them, promote those to better Offices: This will encourage others to procure for themselves such profitable Drubbings, by multiplying and enlarging such Provocations, and *all with work towards the End you aim at.*

XII.   Another Way to make your Tax odious, is to misapply the Produce of it. If it was originally appropriated for the *Defence* of the Provinces and the better Support of Government, and the Administration of

Justice where it may be *necessary*, then apply none of it to that *Defence*, but bestow it where it is *not necessary*, in augmented Salaries or Pensions to every Governor who has distinguished himself by his Enmity to the People, and by calumniating them to their Sovereign. This will make them pay it more unwillingly, and be more apt to quarrel with those that collect it, and those that imposed it, who will quarrel again with them, and all shall contribute to your *main Purpose* of making them *weary of your Government*.

XIII.   If the People of any Province have been accustomed to support their own Governors and Judges to Satisfaction, you are to apprehend that such Governors and Judges may be thereby influenced to treat the People kindly, and to do them Justice. This is another Reason for applying Part of that Revenue in larger Salaries to such Governors and Judges, given, as their Commissions are, *during your Pleasure* only, forbidding them to take any Salaries from their Provinces; that thus the People may no longer hope any Kindness from their Governors, or (in Crown Cases) any Justice from their Judges. And as the Money thus mis-applied in one Province is extorted from all, probably *all will resent the Mis-application*.

XIV.   If the Parliaments of your Provinces should dare to claim Rights or complain of your Administration, order them to be harass'd with repeated *Dissolutions*. If the same Men are continually return'd by new Elections, adjourn their Meetings to some Country Village where they cannot be accommodated, and there keep them *during Pleasure*; for this, you know, is your PREROGATIVE; and an excellent one it is, as you may manage it, to promote Discontents among the

People, diminish their Respect, and *increase their Dis-affection.*

XV.   Convert the brave honest Officers of your Navy into pimping Tide-waiters and Colony Officers of the Customs. Let those who in Time of War fought gallantly in Defence of the Commerce of their Countrymen, in Peace be taught to prey upon it. Let them learn to be corrupted by great and real Smugglers, but (to shew their Diligence) scour with armed Boats every Bay, Harbour, River, Creek, Cove or Nook throughout the Coast of your Colonies, stop and detain every Coaster, every Wood-boat, every Fisherman, tumble their Cargoes, and even their Ballast, inside out and upside down; and if a Penn'orth of Pins is found un-entered, let the Whole be seized and confiscated. Thus shall the Trade of your Colonists suffer more from their Friends in Time of Peace, than it did from their Enemies in War. Then let these Boats Crews land upon every Farm in their Way, rob the Orchards, steal the Pigs and Poultry, and insult the Inhabitants. If the injured and exasperated Farmers, unable to procure other Justice, should attack the Agressors, drub them and burn their Boats, you are to call this *High Treason* and *Rebellion,* order Fleets and Armies into their Country, and threaten to carry all the Offenders three thousand Miles to be hang'd, drawn and quartered. *O! this will work admirably!*

XVI.   If you are told of Discontents in your Colonies, never believe that they are general, or that you have given Occasion for them; therefore do not think of applying any Remedy, or of changing any offensive Measure. Redress no Grievance, lest they should be encouraged to demand the Redress of some other Grievance. Grant no Request that is just and reasonable, lest they should make another that is unreasonable. Take all your Informations of the State of the Colonies from your Governors and Officers in Enmity with them. Encourage and reward these *Leasing-makers*; secrete their lying Accusations lest they should be confuted; but act upon them as the clearest Evidence, and believe nothing you hear from the Friends of the People. Suppose all *their* Complaints to be invented and promoted by a few factious Demagogues, whom if you could catch and hang, all would be quiet. Catch and hang a few of them accordingly; and the *Blood of the Martyrs* shall *work Miracles* in favour of your Purpose.

XVII. If you see *rival Nations* rejoicing at the Prospect of your Disunion with your Provinces, and endeavouring to promote it: If they translate, publish and applaud all the Complaints of your discontented Colonists, at the same Time privately stimulating you to severer Measures; let not that *alarm* or offend you. Why should it? since you all mean *the same Thing*.

XVIII. If any Colony should at their own Charge erect a Fortress to secure their Port against the Fleets of a foreign Enemy, get your Governor to betray that Fortress into your Hands. Never think of paying what it cost the Country, for that would *look*, at least, like some Regard for Justice; but turn it into a Citadel to awe the Inhabitants and curb their Commerce. If they should have lodged in such Fortress the very Arms they bought and used to aid you in your Conquests, seize them all, 'twill provoke like *Ingratitude* added to *Robbery*. One admirable Effect of these Operations will be, to discourage every other Colony from erecting such Defences, and so their and your

Enemies may more easily invade them, to the great Disgrace of your Government, and of course *the Furtherance of your Project.*

XIX. Send Armies into their Country under Pretence of protecting the Inhabitants; but instead of garrisoning the Forts on their Frontiers with those Troops, to prevent Incursions, demolish those Forts, and order the Troops into the Heart of the Country, that the Savages may be encouraged to attack the Frontiers, and that the Troops may be protected by the Inhabitants: This will seem to proceed from your Ill will or your Ignorance, and contribute farther to produce and strengthen an Opinion among them, *that you are no longer fit to govern them.*

XX. Lastly, Invest the General of your Army in the Provinces with great and unconstitutional Powers, and free him from the Controul of even your own Civil Governors. Let him have Troops enow under his Command, with all the Fortresses in his Possession; and who knows but (like some provincial Generals in the Roman Empire, and encouraged by the universal Discontent you have produced) he may take it into his Head to set up for himself. If he should, and you have carefully practised these few *excellent Rules* of mine, take my Word for it, all the Provinces will immediately join him, and you will that Day (if you have not done it sooner) get rid of the Trouble of governing them, and all the *Plagues* attending their *Commerce* and Connection from thenceforth and for ever.

Q. E. D.

The Public Advertiser, SEPTEMBER 11, 1773

AN EDICT BY THE KING OF PRUSSIA

For the Public Advertiser.
THE SUBJECT of the following Article of
FOREIGN INTELLIGENCE
being exceeding EXTRAORDINARY, is the Reason of its being
separated from the usual Articles of *Foreign News.*

Dantzick, September 5.

WE have long wondered here at the Supineness of the English Nation, under the Prussian Impositions upon its Trade entering our Port. We did not till lately know the *Claims,* antient and modern, that hang over that Nation, and therefore could not suspect that it might submit to those Impositions from a Sense of *Duty,* or from Principles of *Equity.* The following *Edict,* just made public, may, if serious, throw some Light upon this Matter.

'FREDERICK, by the Grace of God, King of *Prussia,* &c. &c. &c. to all present and to come,[*] HEALTH. The Peace now enjoyed throughout our Dominions, having afforded us Leisure to apply ourselves to the Regulation of Commerce, the Improvement of our Finances, and at the same Time the easing our Domestic Subjects in their Taxes: For these Causes, and other good Considerations us thereunto moving, We hereby make known, that after having deliberated these Affairs in our Council,

[*] *A tous presens & à venire.* Orig.

present our dear Brothers, and other great Officers of the State, Members of the same, WE, of our certain Knowledge, full Power and Authority Royal, have made and issued this present Edict, viz.

'WHEREAS it is well known to all the World, that the first German Settlements made in the Island of *Britain*, were by Colonies of People, Subjects to our renowned Ducal Ancestors, and drawn from *their* Dominions, under the Conduct of *Hengist, Horsa, Hella, Uffa, Cerdicus, Ida*, and others; and that the said Colonies have flourished under the Protection of our august House, for Ages past, have never been *emancipated* therefrom, and yet have hitherto yielded little Profit to the same. And whereas We Ourself have in the last War fought for and defended the said Colonies against the Power of *France*, and thereby enabled them to make Conquests from the said Power in *America*, for which we have not yet received adequate Compensation. And whereas it is just and expedient that a Revenue should be raised from the said Colonies in *Britain* towards our Indemnification; and that those who are Descendants of our antient Subjects, and thence still owe us due Obedience, should contribute to the replenishing of our Royal Coffers, as they must have done had their Ancestors remained in the Territories now to us appertaining: WE do therefore hereby ordain and command, That from and after the Date of these Presents, there shall be levied and paid to our Officers of the Customs, on all Goods, Wares and Merchandizes, and on all Grain and other Produce of the Earth exported from the said Island of *Britain*, and on all Goods of whatever Kind imported into the same, a *Duty* of *Four and an Half* per Cent. *ad Valorem*, for the Use of us and our Successors.— And that the said Duty may more effectually be collected, We do hereby ordain, that all Ships or Vessels bound from *Great Britain* to any other Part of the World, or from any other Part of the World to *Great Britain*, shall in their respective Voyages touch at our Port of KONINGSBERG, there to be unladen, searched, and charged with the said Duties.

'And WHEREAS there have been from Time to Time discovered in the said Island of *Great Britain* by our Colonists there, many Mines or Beds of Iron Stone; and sundry Subjects of our antient Dominion, skilful in converting the said Stone into Metal, have in Times past transported themselves thither, carrying with them and communicating that Art; and the Inhabitants of the said Island, *presuming* that they had a natural Right to make the best Use they could of the natural Productions of their Country for their own Benefit, have not only built Furnaces for smelting the said Stone into Iron, but have erected Plating Forges, Slitting Mills, and Steel Furnaces, for the more convenient manufacturing of the same, thereby endangering a Diminution of the said Manufacture in our antient Dominion. WE *do therefore* hereby farther ordain, that from and after the Date hereof, no Mill or other Engine for Slitting or Rolling of Iron, or any Plating Forge to work with a Tilt-Hammer, or any Furnace for making Steel, shall be erected or continued in the said Island of *Great Britain*: And the Lord Lieutenant of every County in the said Island is hereby commanded, on Information of any such Erection within his County, to order and by Force to cause the same to be abated and destroyed, as he shall answer the Neglect thereof to Us at his Peril.—But We are nevertheless graciously pleased to permit the Inhabitants of the said Island to transport their Iron into *Prussia*, there to be manufactured, and to them returned, they paying our Prussian Subjects for the Workmanship, with all the Costs of Commission, Freight and Risque coming and returning, any Thing herein contained to the contrary notwithstanding.

'WE do not however think fit to extend this our Indulgence to the Article of *Wool*, but meaning to encourage not only the manufacturing of woollen Cloth, but also the raising of Wool in our antient Dominions, and to prevent *both*, as much as may be, in our said Island, We do hereby absolutely forbid the Transportation of Wool from thence even to the Mother Country *Prussia*; and that those Islanders may be farther and more effectually restrained in making any Advantage of their own Wool in the Way of Manufacture, We command that none shall be carried *out of one County into another*, nor shall any Worsted-Bay, or Woollen-Yarn, Cloth, Says, Bays, Kerseys, Serges, Frizes, Druggets, Cloth-Serges, Shalloons, or any other Drapery Stuffs, or Woollen Manufactures whatsoever, made up or mixt with Wool in any of the said Counties, be carried into any other County, or be Water-borne even across the smallest River or Creek, on Penalty of Forfeiture of the same, together with the Boats, Carriages, Horses, &c. that shall be employed in removing them. *Nevertheless* Our loving Subjects there are hereby permitted, (if they think proper) to use all their Wool as *Manure for the Improvement of their Lands*.

'AND WHEREAS the Art and Mystery of making *Hats* hath arrived at great Perfection in *Prussia*, and the making of Hats by our remote Subjects ought to be as much as possible restrained. And forasmuch as the Islanders before-mentioned, being in Possession of Wool, Beaver, and other Furs, have *presumptuously* conceived they had a Right to make some Advantage thereof, by manufacturing the same into Hats, to the

Prejudice of our domestic Manufacture, WE do therefore hereby strictly command and ordain, that no Hats or Felts whatsoever, dyed or undyed, finished or unfinished, shall be loaden or put into or upon any Vessel, Cart, Carriage or Horse, to be transported or conveyed *out of one County* in the said Island *into another County*, or to a*ny other Place whatsoever*, by any Person or Persons whatsoever, on Pain of forfeiting the same, with a Penalty of *Five Hundred Pounds* Sterling for every Offence. Nor shall any Hat-maker in any of the said Counties employ more than two Apprentices, on Penalty of *Five Pounds* Sterling per Month: We intending hereby that such Hat-makers, being so restrained both in the Production and Sale of their Commodity, may find no Advantage in continuing their Business.—But lest the said Islanders should suffer Inconveniency by the Want of Hats, We are farther graciously pleased to permit them to send their Beaver Furs to *Prussia*; and We also permit Hats made thereof to be exported from *Prussia* to *Britain*, the People thus favoured to pay all Costs and Charges of Manufacturing, Interest, Commission to Our Merchants, Insurance and Freight going and returning, as in the Case of Iron.

'And lastly, Being willing farther to favour Our said Colonies in *Britain*, We do hereby also ordain and command, that all the Thieves, Highway and Street-Robbers, House-breakers, Forgerers, Murderers, So——tes, and Villains of every Denomination, who have forfeited their Lives to the Law in *Prussia*, but whom We, in Our great Clemency, do not think fit here to hang, shall be emptied out of our Gaols into the said Island of *Great Britain* for the BETTER PEOPLING *of that Country*.

'We flatter Ourselves that these Our Royal Regulations and

Commands will be thought *just* and *reasonable* by Our much-favoured Colonists in *England*, the said Regulations being copied from their own Statutes of 10 and 11 Will. III. C. 10.—5 Geo. II. C. 22.—23 Geo. II. C. 29.—4 Geo. I. C. 11. and from other equitable Laws made by their Parliaments, or from Instructions given by their Princes, or from Resolutions of both Houses entered into for the GOOD *Government* of their own Colonies in *Ireland* and *America*.

'And all Persons in the said Island are hereby cautioned not to oppose in any wise the Execution of this Our Edict, or any Part thereof, such Opposition being HIGH TREASON, of which all who are *suspected* shall be transported in Fetters from *Britain* to *Prussia*, there to be tried and executed according to the *Prussian Law*.

    'Such is our Pleasure.

        'Given at *Potsdam* this twenty-fifth Day of the Month of August, One Thousand Seven Hundred and Seventy-three, and in the Thirty-third Year of our Reign. '

        By the KING in his Council.

            'RECHTMÆSSIG, *Secr.*'

Some take this Edict to be merely one of the King's *Jeux d'Esprit*: Others suppose it serious, and that he means a Quarrel with England: But all here think the Assertion it concludes with, "that these Regulations are copied from Acts of the English Parliament respecting their Colonies," a very *injurious* one: it being impossible to believe, that a People distinguished for their *Love of Liberty*, a Nation so *wise*, so *liberal in its Sentiments*, so *just and equitable* towards its *Neighbours*, should, from mean and *injudicious* Views of *petty immediate Profit*, treat *its own Children* in a Manner so *arbitrary* and TYRANNICAL!

The Public Advertiser, SEPTEMBER 22, 1773

"A WAR IT WILL BE"

To the Printer of the Publick Ledger

SIR,

Nothing can equal the present Rage of our Ministerial Writers against our Brethren in America, who have the Misfortune to be *Whigs* in a Reign when *Whiggism* is out of Fashion, who are besides Protestant Dissenters and Lovers of Liberty. One may easily see from what Quarter comes the Abuse of those People in the Papers; their Struggle for their Rights is called REBELLION, and the People REBELS; while those who really rebell'd in Scotland (1745) for the Expulsion of the present reigning Family, and the Establishment of Popery and arbitrary Power on the Ruins of Liberty and Protestantism; who enter'd England, and trampled on its Belly as far as Derby, to the Astonishment of this great City and shaking the publick Credit of the Nation; have now all their Sins forgiven on Account of their modish Principles, and are called not *Rebels*, but by the softer Appellation of *Insurgents*!

These angry Writers use their utmost Efforts to persuade us that this War with the Colonies (for a War it will be) is a *national* Cause when in fact it is merely a *ministerial* one. Administration wants an American Revenue to dissipate in Corruption. The Quarrel is about a paltry three-penny Duty on Tea. There is no real Clashing of Interests between Britain and America. Their Commerce is to their mutual Advantage, or rather most to the Advantage of Britain, which finds a vast Market in America for its Manufactures; and *as good Pay*, I speak from Knowledge, as in any Country she trades to upon the Face of the Globe. But the Fact needs not my Testimony, it speaks for it self; for if we could elsewhere get better Pay and better Prices, we should not send our Goods to America. The gross Calumniators of that People, who want us to imbrue our Hands in Brother's Blood, have the Effrontery to tell the World that the Americans associated in Resolutions not to pay us what they ow'd us unless we repeal'd the Stamp Act. This is an INFAMOUS FALSHOOD; they know it to be such. I call upon the Incendiaries who have advanc'd it, to produce their Proofs. Let them name any two that enter'd into such an Association, or any one that made such a Declaration. Absurdity marks the very Face of this Lie. Every one acquainted with Trade knows, that a credited Merchant daring to be concern'd in such an Association, could never expect to be trusted again. His Character on the Exchange of London would be ruined forever. The great Credit given them since that time, nay the present Debt due from them, is itself a Proof of the Confidence we have in their Probity.

Another villainous Falshood advanc'd against the Americans is, that tho' we have been at such Expence in protecting them, they refuse to contribute their Part to the publick general Expence of the Empire. The Fact is, that *they never did refuse a Requisition of that kind*. A Writer who calls himself *Sagittarius* (I suppose from his flinging about, like Solomon's Fool, Firebrands, *Arrows* and Death) in the Ledger of March 9. asserts that the "Experiment has been tried and that they did not think it expedient to return even an Answer." How does he prove this? Why, "the Colony Agents were told by Mr. Grenville, that a Revenue *would be* required from them to defray the Expences of their Protection." But was the Requisition ever made? Were circular Letters ever sent by his Majesty's Command from the Secretary of State to the several Colony Governments, according to the establish'd Custom, stating the Occasion, and requiring such Supplies as were suitable to their Abilities and Loyalty? And did they then refuse not only Compliance but an Answer? No such Matter. Agents are not the Channel thro' which Requisitions are made. If they were told by Mr. Grenville that a "Revenue *would be* required, and yet the Colonies made no Offer, no Grant nor laid any Tax," Does it follow they would not have done it if they had been required? Probably they thought it time enough when the *Requisition* should come, and in fact it never appeared there to this day. In the last War they all gave so liberally, that we thought ourselves bound in honour to return them a Million. But We are disgusted with their Free Gifts; we want to have something that is obtain'd by Force; like a mad Landlord who should refuse the willing Payment of his full Rents, and chuse to take less by way of Robbery.

This shameless Writer, would cajole the People of England, with the Fancy of their being Kings of America, and that their Honour is at Stake by the Americans disputing *their* Government. He thrusts us into the Throne cheek-by-Jole with Majesty, and would have us talk as he writes, of *our* Subjects in America, and *our* Sovereignty over America. Forgetting that the Americans are Subjects of the King, not *our* Subjects, but our *Fellow-Subjects*; and that they have Parliaments of their own, with the Right of granting their own Money by their own Representatives, which we cannot deprive them of but by Violence and Injustice.

Having by a Series of iniquitous and irritating Measures provoked a loyal People almost to Desperation, we now magnify every Act of an American Mob, into REBELLION, tho' the Government there disapprove it and order Prosecution, as is now the Case with regard to the Tea destroyed: And we talk of nothing but Troops and Fleets, and Force, of blocking up Ports, destroying Fisheries, abolishing Charters, &c. &c. Here Mobs of English Sawyers can burn Sawmills; Mobs of English Labourers destroy or plunder Magazines of Corn; Mobs of English Coalheavers attack Houses with Fire Arms; English Smuglers can fight regularly the King's Cruizing Vessels, drive them ashore and burn them, as lately on the Coast of Wales, and on the Coast of Cornwall; but upon these Accounts we hear no Talk of England's being in *Rebellion;* no Threats of taking away its Magna Charta, or repealing its Bill of Rights; For we well know that the Operations of a Mob are often unexpected, sudden, and soon over, so that the Civil Power can seldom prevent or suppress them, not being able to come in before they have dispers'd themselves: And therefore it is not always accountable for their Mischiefs.

Surely the great Commerce of this Nation with the Americans is of too much Importance to be risk'd in a Quarrel which has no Foundation but ministerial Pique and Obstinacy! To us, in the Way of Trade, comes now, and has long come, all the superlucration arising from their Labour. But Will Our reviling them as Cheats, Hypocrites, Scoundrels, Traitors, Cowards, Tyrants, &c. according to the present Court Mode in all our Papers, make them more our Friends, more fond of our Merchandize? Did ever any Tradesman succeed who attempted to drub Customers into his Shop? And Will honest JOHN BULL the Farmer be long satisfy'd with Servants that before his Face attempt to kill his *Plow-Horses*?

A Londoner.

AFTER MARCH 9, 1774

THE SALE OF THE HESSIANS

FROM THE COUNT DE SCHAUMBERGH TO THE BARON
HOHENDORF, COMMANDING THE HESSIAN TROOPS
IN AMERICA

ROME, FEBRUARY 18, 1777.

MONSIEUR LE BARON: —On my return from Naples, I received at Rome your letter of the 27th December of last year. I have learned with unspeakable pleasure the courage our troops exhibited at Trenton, and you cannot imagine my joy on being told that of the 1,950 Hessians engaged in the fight, but 345 escaped. There were just 1,605 men killed, and I cannot sufficiently commend your prudence in sending an exact list of the dead to my minister in London. This precaution was the more necessary, as the report sent to the English ministry does not give but 1,455 dead. This would make 483,450 florins instead of the 643,500 which I am entitled to demand under our convention. You will comprehend the prejudice which such an error would work in my finances, and I do not doubt you will take the necessary pains to prove that Lord North's list is false and yours correct.

The court of London objects that there were a hundred wounded who ought not to be included in the list, nor paid for as dead; but I trust you will not overlook my instructions to you on quitting Cassel, and that you will not have tried by human succor to recall to life the unfortunates whose days could not be lengthened but by the loss of a leg or an arm. That would be making them a pernicious present, and I am sure they would rather die than live in a condition no longer fit for my service. I do not mean by this that you should assassinate them; we should be humane, my dear Baron, but you may insinuate to the surgeons with entire propriety that a crippled man is a reproach to their profession, and that there is no wiser course than to let every one of them die when he ceases to be fit to fight.

I am about to send you some new recruits. Don't economize them. Remember glory before all things. Glory is true wealth. There is nothing degrades the soldier like the love of money. He must care only for honor and reputation, but this reputation must be acquired in the midst of dangers. A battle gained without costing the conqueror any blood is an inglorious success, while the conquered cover themselves with glory by perishing with their arms in their hands. Do you remember that of the 300 Lacedæmonians who defended the defile of Thermopylæ, not

POLITICAL WRITINGS & SATIRES

one returned? How happy should I be could I say the same of my brave Hessians!

It is true that their king, Leonidas, perished with them: but things have changed, and it is no longer the custom for princes of the empire to go and fight in America for a cause with which they have no concern. And besides, to whom should they pay the thirty guineas per man if I did not stay in Europe to receive them? Then, it is necessary also that I be ready to send recruits to replace the men you lose. For this purpose I must return to Hesse. It is true, grown men are becoming scarce there, but I will send you boys. Besides, the scarcer the commodity, the higher the price. I am assured that the women and little girls have begun to till our lands, and they get on not badly. You did right to send back to Europe that Dr. Crumerus who was so successful in curing dysentery. Don't bother with a man who is subject to looseness of the bowels. That disease makes bad soldiers. One coward will do more mischief in an engagement than ten brave men will do good. Better that they burst in their barracks than fly in a battle, and tarnish the glory of our arms. Besides, you know that they pay me as killed for all who die from disease, and I don't get a farthing for runaways. My trip to Italy, which has cost me enormously, makes it desirable that there should be a great mortality among them. You will therefore promise promotion to all who expose themselves; you will exhort them to seek glory in the midst of dangers; you will say to Major Maundorff that I am not at all content with his saving the 345 men who escaped the massacre at Trenton. Through the whole campaign he has not had ten men killed in consequence of his orders. Finally, let it be your principal object to prolong the war and avoid a decisive engagement on either side, for I have made arrangements for a grand Italian opera, and I do not wish to be obliged to give it up. Meantime I pray God, my dear Baron de Hohendorf, to have you in his holy and gracious keeping.

SPEECH IN THE CONSTITUTIONAL CONVENTION AT THE CONCLUSION OF ITS DELIBERATIONS

MR. PRESIDENT,

I confess, that I do not entirely approve of this Constitution at present; but, Sir, I am not sure I shall never approve of it: for, having lived long, I have experienced many instances of being obliged, by better information or fuller consideration, to change my opinions even on important subjects, which I once thought right, but found to be otherwise. It is therefore that, the older I grow, the more apt I am to doubt my own judgment, and to pay more respect to the judgment of others. Most men, indeed, as well as most sects in religion, think themselves in possession of all truth, and that whenever others differ from them, it is so far error. Steele, a Protestant, in a dedication, tells the pope, that the only difference between our two churches, in their opinions of the certainty of their doctrine, is, the Romish Church is *infallible*, and the Church of England is *never in the wrong*. But though many private persons think almost as highly of their own infallibility as that of their sect, few express it so naturally as a certain French lady, who, in a little dispute with her sister, said, 'I don't know how it happens, sister, but I meet with nobody but myself who is *always* in the right.'—*Je ne trouve que moi qui aie toujours raison.*"

In these sentiments, Sir, I agree to this Constitution with all its faults,—if they are such; because I think a general Government necessary for us, and there is no *form* of government but what might be a blessing if well administered; and I believe further, that this is likely to be well administered for a course of years, and can only end in desertion as other forms have done before it, when the people shall become so corrupted as to need despotic government, being incapable of any other. I doubt, too, whether any other convention we can obtain may be able to make a better constitution : for when you assemble a number of men to have the advantage of their joint wisdom, you inevitably assemble with those men all their prejudices, their passions, their errors of opinion, their local interests, and their selfish views. From such an assembly can a *perfect* production be expected? It therefore astonishes me, Sir, to find this system approaching so near to perfection as it docs; and I think it will astonish our enemies, who are waiting with confidence to hear that our councils are confounded, like those of the builders of Babel, and that our States are on the point of separation only to meet hereafter for the purpose of cutting each others throats. Thus I consent, Sir, to this because I expect no better, and because I am not sure that this is not the best. The opinions I have bad of its *errors*, I sacrifice to the public good. I have never whispered a syllable of them abroad. Within these walls they were born, and here they shall die. If every one of us, in returning to our constituents, were to report the objections he has had to it, and endeavour to gain partizaus in support of them, we might prevent its being generally received, and therefore lose all the salutary effects and great advantages resulting naturally in our favour among foreign nations, as well as among ourselves from our real apparent unanimity. Much of the strength and efficiency of any government in procuring and securing happiness to the people depends on *opinion*, on the general opinion of the goodness of that government, as well as of the wisdom and integrity of its governors. I hope, therefore, that for our own sakes, as a part of the people, and for the sake of our posterity, we shall act heartily and unanimously in recommending this constitution, wherever our influence may extend, and turn our future thoughts and endeavours to the means of having it *well administered*.

On the whole, Sir, I cannot help expressing'a wish that every member of the convention who may still have objections, would with me on this occasion, doubt a little of his own infallibility, and, to make *manifest* our *unanimity*, put his name to this instrument.

SEPTEMBER 17, 1787

SIDI MEHEMET IBRAHIM ON THE SLAVE TRADE

TO THE EDITOR OF THE FEDERAL GAZETTE

MARCH 23d, 1790.

SIR,

Reading last night in your excellent Paper the speech of Mr. Jackson in Congress against their meddling with the Affair of Slavery, or attempting to mend the Condition of the Slaves, it put me in mind of a similar One made about 100 Years since by Sidi Mehemet Ibrahim, a member of the Divan of Algiers, which may be seen in Martin's Account of his Consulship, anno 1687. It was against granting the Petition of the Sect called *Erika*, or Purists, who prayed for the Abolition of Piracy and Slavery as being unjust. Mr. Jackson does not quote it; perhaps he has not seen it. If, therefore, some of its Reasonings are to be found in his eloquent Speech, it may only show that men's Interests and Intellects operate and are operated on with surprising similarity in all Countries and Climates, when under similar Circumstances. The African's Speech, as translated, is as follows.

> *"Allah Bismillah, &c.*
> *God is great, and Mahomet is his Prophet.*

"Have these *Erika* considered the Consequences of granting their Petition? If we cease our Cruises against the Christians, how shall we be furnished with the Commodities their Countries produce, and which are so necessary for us? If we forbear to make Slaves of their People, who in this hot Climate are to cultivate our Lands? Who are to perform the common Labours of our City, and in our Families? Must we not then be our own Slaves? And is there not more Compassion and more Favour due to us as Mussulmen, than to these Christian Dogs? We have now above 50,000 Slaves in and near Algiers. This Number, if not kept up by fresh Supplies, will soon diminish, and be gradually annihilated. If we then cease taking and plundering the Infidel Ships, and making Slaves of the Seamen and Passengers, our Lands will become of no Value for want of Cultivation; the Rents of Houses in the City will sink one half; and the Revenues of Government arising from its Share of Prizes be totally destroy'd! And for what? To gratify the whims of a whimsical Sect, who would have us, not only forbear making more Slaves, but even to manumit those we have.

"But who is to indemnify their Masters for the Loss? Will the State do it? Is our Treasury sufficient? Will the *Erika* do it? Can they do it? Or would they, to do what they think Justice to the Slaves, do a greater Injustice to the Owners? And if we set our Slaves free, what is to be done with them? Few of them will return to their Countries; they know too well the greater Hardships they must there be subject to; they will not embrace our holy Religion; they will not adopt our Manners; our People will not pollute themselves by intermarrying with them. Must we maintain them as Beggars in our Streets, or suffer our Properties to be the Prey of their Pillage? For Men long accustom'd to Slavery will not work for a Livelihood when not compell'd. And what is there so pitiable in their present Condition? Were they not Slaves in their own Countries?

"Are not Spain, Portugal, France, and the Italian states govern'd by

Despots, who hold all their Subjects in Slavery, without Exception? Even England treats its Sailors as Slaves; for they are, whenever the Government pleases, seiz'd, and confin'd in Ships of War, condemn'd not only to work, but to fight, for small Wages, or a mere Subsistence, not better than our Slaves are allow'd by us. Is their Condition then made worse by their falling into our Hands? No; they have only exchanged one Slavery for another, and I may say a better; for here they are brought into a Land where the Sun of Islamism gives forth its Light, and shines in full Splendor, and they have an Opportunity of making themselves acquainted with the true Doctrine, and thereby saving their immortal Souls. Those who remain at home have not that Happiness. Sending the Slaves home then would be sending them out of Light into Darkness.

"I repeat the Question, What is to be done with them? I have heard it suggested, that they may be planted in the Wilderness, where there is plenty of Land for them to subsist on, and where they may flourish as a free State; but they are, I doubt, too little dispos'd to labour without Compulsion, as well as too ignorant to establish a good government, and the wild Arabs would soon molest and destroy or again enslave them. While serving us, we take care to provide them with every thing, and they are treated with Humanity. The Labourers in their own Country are, as I am well informed, worse fed, lodged, and clothed. The Condition of most of them is therefore already mended, and requires no further Improvement. Here their Lives are in Safety. They are not liable to be impress'd for Soldiers, and forc'd to cut one another's Christian Throats, as in the Wars of their own Countries. If some of the religious mad Bigots, who now teaze us with their silly Petitions, have in a Fit of blind Zeal freed their Slaves, it was not Generosity, it was not Humanity, that mov'd them to the Action; it was from the conscious Burthen of a Load of Sins, and Hope, from the supposed Merits of so good a Work, to be excus'd from Damnation.

"How grossly are they mistaken in imagining Slavery to be disallow'd by the Alcoran! Are not the two Precepts, to quote no more, '*Masters, treat your Slaves with kindness; Slaves, serve your Masters with Cheerfulness and Fidelity,*' clear Proofs to the contrary? Nor can the Plundering of Infidels be in that sacred Book forbidden, since it is well known from it, that God has given the World, and all that it contains, to his faithful Mussulmen, who are to enjoy it of Right as fast as they conquer it. Let us then hear no more of this detestable Proposition, the Manumission of Christian Slaves, the Adoption of which would, by depreciating our Lands and Houses, and thereby depriving so many good Citizens of their Properties, create universal Discontent, and provoke Insurrections, to the endangering of Government and producing general Confusion. I have therefore no doubt, but this wise Council will prefer the Comfort and Happiness of a whole Nation of true Believers to the Whim of a few *Erika*, and dismiss their Petition."

The Result was, as Martin tells us, that the Divan came to this Resolution; "The Doctrine, that Plundering and Enslaving the Christians is unjust, is at best *problematical*; but that it is the Interest of this State to continue the Practice, is clear; therefore let the Petition be rejected."

And it was rejected accordingly.

And since like Motives are apt to produce in the Minds of Men like Opinions and Resolutions, may we not, Mr. Brown, venture to pre-dict, from this Account, that the Petitions to the Parliament of England for abolishing the Slave-Trade, to say nothing of other Legislatures, and the Debates upon them, will have a similar Conclusion? I am, Sir, your constant Reader and humble Servant,

Historicus.

The Federal Gazette, MARCH 25, 1790

LETTERS

TO PETER COLLINSON

I received your Favour of the 29th. August last and thank you for the kind and judicious remarks you have made on my little Piece. Whatever further occurs to you on the same subject, you will much oblige me in communicating it.

I have often observed with wonder, that Temper of the poor English Manufacturers and day Labourers which you mention, and acknowledge it to be pretty general. When any of them happen to come here, where Labour is much better paid than in England, their Industry seems to diminish in equal proportion. But it is not so with the German Labourers; They retain the habitual Industry and Frugality they bring with them, and now receiving higher Wages an accumulation arises that makes them all rich.

When I consider, that the English are the Offspring of Germans, that the Climate they live in is much of the same Temperature; when I can see nothing in Nature that should create this Difference, I am apt to suspect it must arise from Institution, and I have sometimes doubted, whether the Laws peculiar to England which compel the Rich to maintain the Poor, have not given the latter, a Dependance that very much lessens the care of providing against the wants of old Age.

I have heard it remarked that the Poor in Protestant Countries on the Continent of Europe, are generally more industrious than those of Popish Countries, may not the more numerous foundations in the latter for the relief of the poor have some effect towards rendering them less provident. To relieve the misfortunes of our fellow creatures is concurring with the Deity, 'tis Godlike, but if we provide encouragements for Laziness, and supports for Folly, may it not be found fighting against the order of God and Nature, which perhaps has appointed Want and Misery as the proper Punishments for, and Cautions against as well as necessary consequences of Idleness and Extravagancy.

Whenever we attempt to mend the scheme of Providence and to interfere in the Government of the World, we had need be very circumspect lest we do more harm than Good. In New England they once thought Black-birds useless and mischievous to their corn, they made Laws to destroy them, the consequence was, the Black-birds were diminished but a kind of Worms which devoured their Grass, and which the Black-birds had been used to feed on encreased prodigiously; Then finding their Loss in Grass much greater than their saving in corn they wished again for their Black-birds.

We had here some years since a Transylvanian Tartar, who had travelled much in the East, and came hither merely to see the West, intending to go home thro' the spanish West Indies, China &c. He asked me one day what I thought might be the Reason that so many and such numerous nations, as the Tartars in Europe and Asia, the Indians in America, and the Negroes in Africa, continued a wandring careless Life, and refused to live in Cities, and to cultivate the arts they saw practiced by the civilized part of Mankind. While I was considering what answer to make him; I'll tell you, says he in his broken English, God make man for Paradise, he make him for to live lazy; man make God angry, God turn him out of Paradise, and bid him work; man no love work; he want to go to Paradise again, he want to live lazy; so all mankind love lazy. Howe'er this may be it seems certain, that the hope of becoming at some time of Life free from the necessity of care and Labour, together with fear of penury, are the main-springs of most peoples industry.

To those indeed who have been educated in elegant plenty, even the provision made for the poor may appear misery, but to those who have scarce ever been better provided for, such provision may seem quite good and sufficient, these latter have then nothing to fear worse than their present Conditions, and scarce hope for any thing better than a Parish maintainance; so that there is only the difficulty of getting that maintainance allowed while they are able to work, or a little shame they suppose attending it, that can induce them to work at all, and what they do will only be from hand to mouth.

The proneness of human Nature to a life of ease, of freedom from care and labour appears strongly in the little success that has hitherto attended every attempt to civilize our American Indians, in their present way of living, almost all their Wants are supplied by the spontaneous Productions of Nature, with the addition of very little labour, if hunting and fishing may indeed be called labour when Game is so plenty, they visit us frequently, and see the advantages that Arts, Sciences, and compact Society procure us, they are not deficient in natural understanding and yet they have never shewn any Inclination to change their manner of life for ours, or to learn any of our Arts; When an Indian Child has been brought up among us, taught our language and habituated to our Customs, yet if he goes to see his relations and make one Indian Ramble with them, there is no perswading him ever to return, and that this is not natural to them merely as Indians, but as men, is plain from this, that when white persons of either sex have been taken prisoners young by the Indians, and lived a while among them, tho' ransomed by their Friends, and treated with all imaginable tenderness to prevail with them to stay among the English, yet in a Short time they become disgusted with our manner of life, and the care and pains that are necessary to support it, and take the first good Opportunity of escaping again into the Woods, from whence there is no reclaiming them. One instance I remember to have heard, where the person was brought home to possess a good Estate; but finding some care necessary to keep it together, he relinquished it to a younger Brother, reserving to himself nothing but a gun and a match-Coat, with which he took his way again to the Wilderness.

Though they have few but natural wants and those easily supplied. But with us are infinite Artificial wants, no less craving than those of Nature, and much more difficult to satisfy; so that I am apt to imagine that close Societies subsisting by Labour and Arts, arose first not from choice, but from necessity: When numbers being driven by war from their hunting grounds and prevented by seas or by other nations were crowded together into some narrow Territories, which without labour would not afford them Food. However as matters now stand with us, care and industry seem absolutely necessary to our well being; they should therefore have every Encouragement we can invent, and not one Motive to diligence be subtracted, and the support of the Poor should not be by maintaining them in Idleness, But by employing them in some kind of labour suited to their Abilities of body &c. as I am informed of late begins to be the practice in many parts of England, where work houses are erected for that purpose. If these were general I should think the Poor would be more careful and work voluntarily and lay up something for themselves against a rainy day, rather than run the risque of being obliged to work at the pleasure of others for a bare subsistence and that too under confinement. The little value Indians set on what we prize so highly under the name of Learning appears from a pleasant passage that happened some years since at a Treaty between one of our Colonies and the Six Nations; when every thing had been settled to the Satisfaction of both sides, and nothing remained but a mutual exchange of civilities, the English Commissioners told the Indians, they had in their Country a College for the instruction of Youth who were there taught various languages, Arts, and Sciences; that there was a particular foundation in favour of the Indians to defray the expense of the Education of any of their sons who should desire to take the Benefit of it. And now if the Indians would accept of the Offer, the English would take half a dozen of their brightest lads and bring them up in the Best manner; The Indians after consulting on the proposal replied that it was remembered some of their Youths had formerly been educated in that College, but it had been observed that for a long time after they returned to their Friends, they were absolutely good for nothing being neither acquainted with the true methods of killing deer, catching Beaver or surprizing an enemy. The Proposition however, they looked on as a mark of the kindness and good will of the English to the Indian Nations which merited a grateful return; and therefore if the English Gentlemen would send a dozen or two of their Children to Onondago the great Council would take care of their Education, bring them up in really what was the best manner and make men of them.

I am perfectly of your mind, that measures of great Temper are necessary with the Germans: and am not without Apprehensions, that thro' their indiscretion or Ours, or both, great disorders and inconveniences may one day arise among us; Those who come hither are generally of the most ignorant Stupid Sort of their own Nation, and as Ignorance is often attended with Credulity when Knavery would mislead it, and with Suspicion when Honesty would set it right; and as few of the English understand the German Language, and so cannot address them either from the Press or Pulpit, 'tis almost impossible to remove any prejudices they once entertain. Their own Clergy have very little influence over the people; who seem to take an uncommon pleasure in abusing and discharging the Minister on every trivial occasion. Not being used to Liberty, they know not how to make a modest use of it; and as Kolben says of the young Hottentots, that they are not esteemed men till they have shewn their manhood by beating their mothers, so these seem to think themselves not free, till they can feel their liberty in abusing and insulting their Teachers. Thus they are under no restraint of Ecclesiastical Government; They behave, however, submissively enough at present to the Civil Government which I wish they may continue to do: For I remember when they modestly declined intermeddling in our Elections, but now they come in droves, and carry all before them, except in one or two Counties; Few of their children in the Country learn English; they import many Books from Germany; and of the six printing houses in the Province, two are entirely German, two half German half English, and but two entirely English; They have one German News-paper, and one half German. Advertisements intended to be general are now printed in Dutch and English; the Signs in our Streets have inscriptions in both languages, and in some places only German: They begin of late to make all their Bonds and other legal Writings in their own Language, which (though I think it ought not to be) are allowed good in our Courts, where the German Business so encreases that there is continual need of Interpreters; and I suppose in a few years they will be also necessary in the Assembly, to tell one half of our Legislators what the other half say; In short unless the stream of their importation could be turned from this to other Colonies, as you very judiciously propose, they will soon so out number us, that all the advantages we have will not in My Opinion be able to preserve our language, and even our Government will become precarious. The French who watch all advantages, are now themselves making a German settlement back of us in the Ilinoes Country, and by means of those Germans they may in time come to an understanding with ours, and indeed in the last war our Germans shewed a general disposition that seems to bode us no good; for when the English who were not Quakers, alarmed by the danger arising from the defenceless state of our Country entered unanimously into an Association within this Government and the lower Countries raised armed and Disciplined near 10,000 men, the Germans except a very few in proportion to their numbers refused to engage in it, giving out one among another, and even in print, that if they were quiet the French should they take the Country would not molest them; at the same time abusing the Philadelphians for fitting out Privateers against the Enemy; and representing the trouble hazard and Expence of defending the Province, as a greater inconvenience than any that might be expected from a change of Government. Yet I am not for refusing entirely to admit them into our Colonies: all that seems to be necessary is, to distribute them more equally, mix them with the English, establish English Schools where they are now too thick settled, and take some care to prevent the practice lately fallen into by some of the Ship Owners, of sweeping the German Gaols to make up the number of their Passengers. I say I am not against the Admission of Germans in general, for they have their Virtues, their industry and frugality is exemplary; They are excellent husbandmen and contribute greatly to the improvement of a Country.

I pray God long to preserve to Great Britain the English Laws, Manners, Liberties and Religion notwithstanding the complaints so frequent in Your public papers, of the prevailing corruption and degeneracy of your People; I know you have a great deal of Virtue still subsisting among you, and I hope the Constitution is not so near a dissolution, as some seem to apprehend; I do not think you are generally become such Slaves to your Vices, as to draw down that *Justice* Milton speaks of when he says that

      ——sometimes Nations will descend so low
      From reason, which is virtue, that no Wrong,
      But Justice, and some fatal curse annex'd
      Deprives them of their *outward* liberty,
      Their *inward* lost.   Parad: lost.

In history we find that Piety, Public Spirit and military Prowess have their Flows, as well as their ebbs, in every nation, and that the Tide is never so low but it may rise again; But should this dreaded fatal change happen in my time, how should I even in the midst of the Affliction rejoice, if we have been able to preserve those invaluable treasures, and can invite the good among you to come and partake of them! O let not Britain seek to oppress us, but like an affectionate parent endeavour to secure freedom to her children; they may be able one day to assist her in defending her own—Whereas a Mortification begun in the Foot may spread upwards to the destruction of the nobler parts of the Body.

I fear I have already extended this rambling letter beyond your patience, and therefore conclude with requesting your acceptance of the inclosed Pamphlet from Sir Your most humble servant

TO ——

Dear Sir   December 13, 1757

I have read your Manuscrit with some Attention. By the Arguments it contains against the Doctrine of a particular Providence, tho' you allow a general Providence, you strike at the Foundation of all Religion: For without the Belief of a Providence that takes Cognizance of, guards and guides and may favour particular Persons, there is no Motive to Worship a Deity, to fear its Displeasure, or to pray for its Protection. I will not enter into any Discussion of your Principles, tho' you seem to desire it; At present I shall only give you my Opinion that tho' your Reasonings are subtle, and may prevail with some Readers, you will not succeed so as to change the general Sentiments of Mankind on that Subject, and the Consequence of printing this Piece will be a great deal of Odium drawn upon your self, Mischief to you and no Benefit to others. He that spits against the Wind, spits in his own Face. But were you to succeed, do you imagine any Good would be done by it? You yourself may find it easy to live a virtuous Life without the Assistance afforded by Religion; you having a clear Perception of the Advantages of Virtue and the Disadvantages of Vice, and possessing a Strength of Resolution sufficient to enable you to resist common Temptations. But think how great a Proportion of Mankind consists of weak and ignorant Men and Women, and of inexperienc'd and inconsiderate Youth of both Sexes, who have need of the Motives of Religion to restrain them from Vice, to support their Virtue, and retain them in the Practice of it till it becomes *habitual*, which is the great Point for its Security; And perhaps you are indebted to her originally that is to your Religious Education, for the Habits of Virtue upon which you now justly value yourself. You might easily display your excellent Talents of reasoning on a less hazardous Subject, and thereby obtain Rank with our most distinguish'd Authors. For among us, it is not necessary, as among the Hottentots that a Youth to be receiv'd into the Company of Men, should prove his Manhood by beating his Mother. I would advise you therefore not to attempt unchaining the Tyger, but to burn this Piece before it is seen by any other Person, whereby you will save yourself a great deal of Mortification from the Enemies it may raise against you, and perhaps a good deal of Regret and Repentance. If

Men are so wicked as we now see them *with Religion* what would they be if *without* it? I intend this Letter itself as a *Proof* of my Friendship and therefore add no *Professions* of it, but subscribe simply Yours

TO JOHN ALLEYNE

DEAR SIR, AUGUST 9, 1768

You made an Apology to me for not acquainting me sooner with your Marriage. I ought now to make an Apology to you for delaying so long the Answer to your Letter. It was mislaid or hid among my Papers, and much Business put it out of my Mind, or prevented my looking for it and writing when I thought of it. So this Account between us if you please may stand balanced.

I assure you it gave me great Pleasure to hear you were married, and into a Family of Reputation. This I learnt from the Public Papers. The Character you give me of your Bride, (as it includes every Qualification that in the married State conduces to mutual Happiness) is an Addition to that Pleasure. Had you consulted me, as a Friend, on the Occasion, Youth on both sides I should not have thought any Objection. Indeed from the Matches that have fallen under my Observation, I am rather inclined to think that early ones stand the best Chance for Happiness. The Tempers and Habits of young People are not yet become so stiff and uncomplying as when more advanced in Life, they form more easily to each other, and thence many Occasions of Disgust are removed. And if Youth has less of that Prudence that is necessary to manage a Family, yet the Parents and elder Friends of young married Persons are generally at hand to afford their Advice, which amply supplies that Defect; and by early Marriage, Youth is sooner form'd to regular and useful Life, and possibly some of those Accidents Habits or Connections that might have injured either the Constitution or the Reputation, or both, are thereby happily prevented. Particular Circumstances of particular Persons may possibly sometimes make it prudent to delay entering into that State, but in general when Nature has render'd our Bodies fit for it, the Presumption is in Nature's Favour, that she has not judg'd amiss in making us desire it. Late Marriages are often attended too with this farther Inconvenience, that there is not the same Chance the Parents shall live to see their offspring educated. *Late Children*, says the Spanish Proverb, *are early Orphans*: A melancholly Reflection to those whose Case it may be! With us in N. America, Marriages are generally in the Morning of Life, our Children are therefore educated and settled in the World by Noon, and thus our Business being done, we have an Afternoon and Evening of chearful Leisure to our selves, such as your Friend at present enjoys. By these early Marriages we are blest with more Children, and from the Mode among us founded in Nature of every Mother suckling and nursing her own Child, more of them are raised. Thence the swift Progress of Population among us unparallel'd in Europe. In fine, I am glad you are married, and congratulate you cordially upon it. You are now more in the way of becoming a useful Citizen; and you have escap'd the unnatural State of *Celibacy for Life*, the Fate of many here who never intended it, but who having too long postpon'd the Change of their Condition, find at length that 'tis too late to think of it, and So live all their Lives in a Situation that greatly lessens a Man's Value: An odd Volume of a Set of Books, you know, is not worth its proportion of the Set; and what think you of the Usefulness of an odd Half of a Pair of Scissars? It cannot well cut any thing. It may possibly serve to scrape a Trencher.

Pray make my Compliments and best Wishes acceptable to your Spouse. I am old and heavy, and grow a little indolent, or I should ere this have presented them in Person. I shall make but small Use of the old Man's Privilege, that of giving Advice to younger Friends. Treat your Wife always with Respect. It will procure Respect to you, not from her only, but from all that observe it. Never use a slighting Expression to her even in jest; for Slights in Jest after frequent bandyings, are apt to end in angry earnest. Be studious in your Profession, and you will be learned. Be industrious and frugal, and you will be rich. Be sober and temperate and you will be healthy. Be in general virtuous, and you will be happy. At least you will by such Conduct stand the best Chance for such Consequences. I pray God to bless you both, being ever Your truly affectionate Friend.

TO GEORGE WHITEFIELD

I am under continued apprehensions that we may have bad news from America. The sending soldiers to Boston always appeared to me a dangerous step; they could do no good, they might occasion mischief. When I consider the warm resentment of a people who think themselves injured and oppressed, and the common insolence of the soldiery, who are taught to consider that people as in rebellion, I cannot but fear the consequences of bringing them together. It seems like setting up a smith's forge in a magazine of gunpowder. I *see* with you that our affairs are not well managed by our rulers here below; I wish I could *believe* with you, that they are well attended to by those above: I rather suspect, from certain circumstances, that though the general government of the universe is well administered, our particular little affairs are perhaps below notice, and left to take the chance of human prudence or imprudence, as either may happen to be uppermost. It is, however, an uncomfortable thought, and I leave it.

(BEFORE SEPTEMBER 2, 1769)

TO TIMOTHY FOLGER

LOVING KINSMAN,   LONDON, SEPT. 29, 1769

Since my Return from abroad, where I spent part of the Summer, I have received your Favours of June 10 and July 26. The Treasury

Board is still under Adjournment, the Lords and Secretaries chiefly in the Country; but as soon as they meet again, you may depend on my making the Application you desire.

I shall enquire concerning the Affair of your two Townships settled under Massachusetts Grants, and let you know my Sentiments as soon as I can get proper Information. I should imagine that whatever may be determin'd here of the Massachusetts Rights to the Jurisdiction, the private Property of Settlers must remain secure. In general I have no great Opinion of Applications to be made here in such Cases. It is so much the Practice to draw Matters into Length, put the Parties to immense Charge, and tire them out with Delays, that I would never come from America hither with any Affair I could possibly settle there.

Mrs. Stevenson sends her Love, and thanks you for remembring her. She is vex'd to hear that the Box of Spermaceti Candles is seiz'd; and says, if ever she sees you again, she will put you in a way of making Reprisals. You know she is a Smuggler upon Principle; and she does not consider how averse you are to every thing of the kind. I thank you for your kind Intention. Your Son grows a fine Youth; he is so obliging as to be with us a little when he has Holidays; and Temple is not the only one of the Family that is fond of his Company.

It gives me great Pleasure to hear that our People are steady in their Resolutions of Non Importation, and in the Promoting of Industry among themselves. They will soon be sensible of the Benefit of such Conduct, tho' the Acts should never be repeal'd to their full Satisfaction. For their Earth and their Sea, the true Sources of Wealth and Plenty, will go on producing; and if they receive the annual Increase, and do not waste it as heretofore in the Gewgaws of this Country, but employ their spare time in manufacturing Necessaries for themselves, they must soon be out of debt, they must soon be easy and comfortable in their circumstances, and even wealthy. I have been told, that in some of our County Courts heretofore, there were every quarter several hundred actions of debt, in which the people were sued by Shopkeepers for money due for British *goods* (as they are called, but in fact *evils*). What a loss of time this must occasion to the people, besides the expense. And how can Freeman bear the thought of subjecting themselves to the hazard of being deprived of their personal liberty at the caprice of every petty trader, for the paltry vanity of tricking out himself and family in the flimsy manufactures of Britain, when they might by their own industry and ingenuity, appear in *good substantial honourable homespun!* Could our folks but see what numbers of Merchants, and even Shopkeepers here, make great estates by American folly; how many shops of A, B, C and Co. with wares for *exportation to the Colonies*, maintain, each shop three or four partners and their families, every one with his country-house and equipage, where they live like Princes on the sweat of our brows; pretending indeed, *sometimes*, to wish well to our Privileges, but on the present important occasion *few* of them affording us any assistance: I am persuaded that indignation would supply our want of prudence, we should disdain the thraldom we have so long been held in by this mischievous commerce, reject it for ever, and seek our resources where God and Nature have placed them WITHIN OUR SELVES.

Your Merchants, on the other hand, have shown a noble *disinterestedness* and *love to their country*, unexampled among Traders in any other age or nation, and which does them infinite honour all over Europe. The corrupted part indeed of this people *here* can scarce believe such virtue possible. But perseverance will convince them, that there is still in the world such a thing as public spirit. I hope that, if the oppressive Acts are not repealed this winter, your Stocks, that us'd to be employed in the British Trade, will be turned to the employment of Manufactures among yourselves: For notwithstanding the former general opinion that manufactures were impracticable in America, on account of the dearness of labour, experience shows, in the success of the manufactures of paper and stockings in Pennsylvania, and of womens shoes *at Lynn* in your province, that labour is only dear *from the want of* CONSTANT *employment*; (he who is often out of work requiring necessarily as much for the time he does work, as will maintain him when he does not work:) and that where we do not *interrupt that employment* by importations, the *cheapness of our provisions* gives us such advantage over the Manufacturers in Britain, that (especially in bulky goods, whose freight would be considerable) *we may always* UNDERWORK THEM.

TO WILLIAM STRAHAN

DEAR SIR, CRAVEN STREET, NOV. 29, 1769

Being just return'd to Town from a little Excursion I find yours of the 22d, containing a Number of Queries that would require a Pamphlet to answer them fully. You however desire only brief Answers, which I shall endeavour to give you. Previous to your Queries, You tell me, that "you apprehend his Majesty's Servants have now in Contemplation; 1st. to releive the Colonists from the Taxes complained of: and 2dly to preserve the Honour, the Dignity, and the Supremacy of the British Legislature over all his Majesty's Dominions." I hope your Information is good, and that what you suppose to be in Contemplation will be carried into Execution, by repealing *all the Laws* that have been made for raising a Revenue in America by Authority of Parliament, without the consent of the People there. The *Honour* and *Dignity* of the British Legislature will not be hurt by such an Act of Justice and Wisdom: The wisest Councils are liable to be misled, especially in Matters remote from their Inspection. It is the persisting in an Error, not the Correcting it that lessens the Honour of any Man or body of Men. The *Supremacy* of that Legislature, I believe will be best preserv'd by making a very sparing use of it, never but for the Evident Good of the Colonies themselves, or of the whole British Empire; never for the Partial Advantage of Britain to their Prejudice; by such Prudent Conduct I imagine that Supremacy may be gradually strengthened and in time fully Established; but otherwise I apprehend it will be disputed, and lost in the Dispute. At present the Colonies consent and Submit to it for the regulation of General Commerce: But a Submission to Acts of Parliament was no part of their original Constitution. Our former Kings Governed their Colonies, as they Governed their Dominions in France, without the Participation of British Parliaments. The Parliament of England never presum'd to interfere with that prerogative till the Time of the Great Rebellion, when they usurp'd the Government of all the King's other Dominions, Ireland, Scotland &c. The Colonies that held for the King, they conquered by Force of Arms, and Governed afterward as Conquered Countries. But New England having not oppos'd the Parliament, was considered and treated as a Sister Kingdom in Amity with England; as appears by the Journals, Mar. 10. 1642.

Your first Question is,

"1. Will not a Repeal of all the Duties (that on Tea excepted, which was before paid here on Exportation, and of Course no new Imposition) fully satisfy the Colonists?"

I think not.

"2. Your Reasons for that Opinion?"

Because it is not *the Sum* paid in that Duty on Tea that is Complain'd of as a Burthen, but the Principle of the Act express'd in the Preamble, viz. that those Duties were laid for the Better Support of Government and the Administration of Justice in the Colonies. This the Colonists think *unnecessary*, *unjust*, and *dangerous* to their Most Important Rights. *Unnecessary*, because in all the Colonies (two or three new ones excepted) Government and the Administration of Justice were and always had been well supported without any Charge to Britain; *Unjust* as it made such Colonies liable to pay such Charge for other Colonies, in which they had no Concern or Interest; *dangerous*, as such a Mode of raising Money for these Purposes, tended to render their Assemblies useless: For if a Revenue could be rais'd in the Colonies for all the purposes of Government, by Act of Parliament, without Grants from the People there, Governors, who do not generally love Assemblies, would never call them, they would be laid aside; and when nothing Should depend upon the People's good will to Government, their Rights would be trampled on, they would be treated with Contempt. Another Reason why I think they would not be satisfy'd with such a partial repeal, is, that their Agreements not to import till the Repeal takes place, include the whole, which shows that they object to the whole; and those Agreements will continue binding on them if the whole is not repealed.

"3. Do you think the only effectual Way of composing the present Differences, is, to put the Americans precisely in the Situation they were in before the passing of the late Stamp Act?"

I think so.

"4. Your Reasons for that Opinion?"

Other Methods have been tryed. They have been rebuked in angry Letters. Their Petitions have been refused or rejected by Parliament. They have been threatened with the Punishments of Treason by Resolves of both Houses. Their Assemblies have been dissolv'd, and Troops have been sent among them; but all these Ways have only exasperated their Minds and widen'd the Breach; their Agreements to use no more British Manufactures have been Strengthen'd, and these Measures instead of composing Differences and promoting a good Correspondence, have almost annihilated your Commerce with those Countries, and greatly endanger'd the National Peace and general Welfare.

"5. If this last Method is deemed by the Legislature and his Majisty's Ministers to be repugnant to their Duty as Guardians of the just Rights of the Crown, and of their Fellow Subjects, can you suggest any other Way of terminating these Disputes, consistent with the Ideas of Justice and propriety conceived by the Kings Subjects on both Sides the Atlantick?"

A. I do not see how that method can be deemed repugnant *to the*

Rights of the Crown. If the Americans are put into their former Situation, it must be by an Act of Parliament, in the Passing of which by the King the Rights of the Crown are exercised not infringed. It is indifferent to the Crown whether the Aids received from America are Granted by Parliament here, or by the Assemblies there, provided the Quantum be the same; and it is my Opinion more will generally be Granted there Voluntarily than can ever be exacted and collected from thence by Authority of parliament. As to the rights of *Fellow Subjects* (I suppose you mean the People of Britain) I cannot conceive how they will be infringed by that method. They will still enjoy the Right of Granting their own money; and may still, if it pleases them, keep up their Claim to the Right of granting ours; a Right they can never exercise properly, for want of a sufficient Knowledge of us, our Circumstances and Abilities (to say nothing of the little likelihood there is that we should ever submit to it) therefore a Right that can be of no good use to them. And we shall continue to enjoy, *in fact*, the Right of granting our own Money; with the Opinion now universally prevailing among us that we are free Subjects of the King, and that *Fellow Subjects* of one Part of his Dominions are not Sovereign over *Fellow Subjects* in any other Part. If the Subjects on the different Sides of the Atlantic, have different and opposite Ideas of Justice or Propriety, no one Method can possibly be consistent with both. The best will be to let each enjoy their own Opinions, without disturbing them when they do not interfere with the common Good.

"6. And if this Method were actually followed do you not think it would encourage the Violent and Factious Part of the Colonists to aim at still farther Concessions from the Mother Country?"

A. I do not think it would. There may be a few among them that deserve the Name of factious and Violent, as there are in all Countries, but these would have little influence if the great Majority of Sober reasonable People were satisfy'd. If any Colony should happen to think that some of your regulations of Trade are inconvenient to the general Interest of the Empire, or prejudicial to them without being beneficial to you, they will state these Matters to the Parliament in Petitions as heretofore, but will, I believe, take no violent steps to obtain, what they may hope for in time from the Wisdom of Government here. I know of nothing else they can have in View. The Notion that prevails here of their being desirous of setting up a Kingdom or Common Wealth of their own, is to my certain Knowledge entirely groundless. I therefore think that on a total Repeal of all Duties laid expressly for the purpose of raising a Revenue on the People of America, without their Consent, the present Uneasiness would subside; the Agreements not to import would be dissolved, and the Commerce flourish as heretofore. And I am confirm'd in this Sentiment by all the Letters I have received from America, and by the Opinion of all the Sensible People who have lately come from thence, Crown Officers excepted. I know indeed that the people of Boston are grievously offended by the Quartering of Troops among them, as they think, contrary to Law; and are very angry with the Board of Commissioners to have calumniated them to Government; but as I suppose withdrawing of those Troops may be a Consequence of Reconciliating Measures taking Place; and that the Commission also will either be dissolv'd if found useless, or fill'd with more temporate and prudent Men if still deemed useful and necessary, I do not imagine these Particulars will prevent a return of the Harmony so much to be wished.

"7. If they are relieved in Part only, what do you, as a reasonable and dispassionate Man, and an equal Friend to both sides, imagine will be the probable Consequence?"

A. I imagine that repealing the offensive Duties in part will answer no End to this Country; the Commerce will remain obstructed, and the Americans go on with their Schemes of Frugality, Industry and Manufactures, to their own great Advantage. How much that may tend to the prejudice of Britain I cannot say; perhaps not so much as some apprehend, since she may in time find New Markets. But I think (if the Union of the two Countries continues to subsist) it will not hurt the *general* interest; for whatever Wealth Britain loses by the Failure of its Trade with the Colonies, America will gain; and the Crown will receive equal Aids from its Subjects upon the whole, if not greater.

And now I have answered your Questions as to what *may* be in my Opinion the Consequences of this or that *supposed* Measure, I will go a little farther, and tell you what I fear is more likely to come to pass *in Reality.*

I apprehend, that the Ministry, at least the American part of it, being fully persuaded of the Right of Parliament, think it ought to be enforc'd whatever may be the Consequences; and at the same time do not believe there is even now any Abatement of the Trade between the two Countries on account of these Disputes; or that if there is, it is small and cannot long Continue; they are assured by the Crown officers in America that Manufactures are impossible there; that the Discontented are few, and Persons of little Consequence; that almost all the People of Property and Importance are satisfyd, and disposed to submit quietly to the Taxing-Power of Parliament; and that if the Revenue Acts are

continued, those Duties only that are called anti-commercial being repealed, and others perhaps laid in their stead, that Power will ere long
be patiently submitted to, and the Agreements not to import be broken
when they are found to produce no Change of Measures here. From these
and similar Misinformations, which seem to be credited, I think it likely
that no thorough redress of Grievances will be afforded to America this
Session. This may inflame Matters still more in that Country; farther rash
Measures there may create more Resentment here, that may Produce not
merely ill-advis'd and useless Dissolutions of their Assemblies, as last
Year; but Attempts to Dissolve their Constitutions; more Troops may be
sent over, which will create more Uneasiness; to justify the Measures of
Government your Ministerial Writers will revile the Americans in your
Newspapers, as they have already began to do, treating them as Miscre-
ants, Rogues, Dastards, Rebels, &c. which will tend farther to alienate
the Minds of the People here from them, and diminish their Affections to
this Country. Possibly too, some of their warm patriots may be distracted
enough to expose themselves by some mad Action, to be sent for Hither,
and Government here be indiscreet enough to Hang them on the Act of
H. 8. Mutual Provocations will thus go on to complete the Separation;
and instead of that cordial Affection that once and so long existed, and
that Harmony so suitable to the Circumstances, and so Necessary to the
Happiness, Strength Safety and Welfare of both Countries; an implacable
Malice and Mutual Hatred, (such as we now see subsisting between the
Spaniards and Portuguese, the Genoese and Corsicans, from the same
Original Misconduct in the Superior Government) will take place; the
Sameness of Nation, the Similarity of Religion, Manners and Language

not in the least Preventing in our Case, more than it did in theirs. I hope however that this may all prove false Prophecy: And that you and I may live to see as sincere and Perfect a friendship establish'd between our respective Countries as has so many years Subsisted between Mr. Strahan and his truly affectionate Friend

TO SAMUEL COOPER

DEAR SIR,   LONDON, JUNE 8, 1770

I received duly your Favour of March 28. With this I send you two Speeches in Parliament on our Affairs by a Member that you know. The Repeal of the whole late Act would undoubtedly have been a prudent Measure, and I have reason to believe that Lord North was for it, but some of the other Ministers could not be brought to agree to it. So the Duty on Tea, with that obnoxious Preamble, remains to continue the Dispute. But I think the next Session will hardly pass over without repealing them; for the Parliament must finally comply with the Sense of the Nation. As to the Standing Army kept up among us in time of Peace, without the Consent of our Assemblies, I am clearly of Opinion that it is not agreable to the Constitution. Should the King by the Aid of his Parliaments in Ireland and the Colonies, raise an Army and bring it into England, quartering it here in time of Peace without the Consent of the Parliament of Great Britain, I am persuaded he would soon be told that he had no Right so to do, and the Nation would ring with Clamours against it. I own that I see no Difference in the Cases. And while we continue so many distinct and separate States, our having the same Head or Sovereign, the King, will not justify such an Invasion of the separate Right of each State to be consulted on the Establishment of whatever Force is proposed to be kept up within its Limits, and to give or refuse its Consent as shall appear most for the Public Good of that State. That the Colonies originally were constituted distinct States, and intended to be continued such, is clear to me from a thorough Consideration of their original Charters, and the whole Conduct of the Crown and Nation towards them until the Restoration. Since that Period, the Parliament here has usurp'd an Authority of making Laws for them, which before it had not. We have for some time submitted to that Usurpation, partly thro' Ignorance and Inattention, and partly from our Weakness and Inability to contend. I hope when our Rights are better understood here, we shall, by a prudent and proper Conduct be able to obtain from the Equity of this Nation a Restoration of them. And in the mean time I could wish that such Expressions as, *The supreme Authority of Parliament; The Subordinacy of our Assemblies to the Parliament* and the like (which in Reality mean nothing if our Assemblies with the King have a true Legislative Authority) I say, I could wish that such Expressions were no more seen in our publick Pieces. They are too strong for Compliment, and tend to confirm a Claim of Subjects in one Part of the King's Dominions to be Sovereigns over their Fellow-Subjects in another Part of his Dominions; when in truth they have no such Right, and their Claim is founded only on Usurpation, the several States having equal Rights and Liberties, and being only connected, as England and Scotland were before the Union, by having one common Sovereign, the King. This kind of Doctrine the Lords and Commons here would deem little less than Treason against what they think their Share of the Sovereignty over the Colonies. To me those Bodies seem to have been long encroaching on the Rights of their and our Sovereign, assuming too much of his Authority, and betraying his Interests. By our Constitutions he is, with his Plantation Parliaments, the sole Legislator of his American Subjects, and in that Capacity is and ought to be free to exercise his own Judgment unrestrain'd and unlimited by his Parliament here. And our Parliaments have Right to grant him Aids without the Consent of this Parliament, a Circumstance which, by the way begins to give it some Jealousy. Let us therefore hold fast our Loyalty to our King (who has the best Disposition towards us, and has a Family-Interest in our Prosperity) as that steady Loyalty is the most probable Means of securing us from the arbitrary Power of a corrupt Parliament, that does not like us, and conceives itself to have an Interest in keeping us down and fleecing us. If they should urge the *Inconvenience* of an Empire's being divided into so many separate States, and from thence conclude that we are not so divided; I would answer, that an Inconvenience proves nothing but itself. England and Scotland were once separate States, under the same King. The Inconvenience found in their being separate States, did not prove that the Parliament of England had a Right to govern Scotland. A formal Union was thought necessary, and England was an hundred Years soliciting it, before she could bring it about. If Great Britain now thinks such an Union necessary with us, let her propose her Terms, and we may consider of them. Were the general Sentiments of this Nation to be consulted in the Case, I should hope the

Terms, whether practicable or not, would at least be equitable: for I think that except among those with whom the Spirit of Toryism prevails, the popular Inclination here is, to wish us well, and that we may preserve our Liberties.

I unbosom my self thus to you in Confidence of your Prudence, and wishing to have your Sentiments on the Subject in Return.

Mr. Pownall, I suppose, will acquaint you with the Event of his Motions, and therefore I say nothing more of them, than that he appears very sincere in his Endeavours to serve us; on which Account I some time since republish'd with Pleasure the parting Addresses to him of your Assembly, with some previous Remarks, to his Honour as well as in Justification of our People.

I hope that before this time those detestable Murderers have quitted your Province, and that the Spirit of Industry and Frugality continues and increases. With sincerest Esteem and Affection, I am, Dear Sir, Your most obedient and most humble Servant

P.S. Just before the last Session of Parliament commenced a Friend of mine, who had Connections with some of the Ministry, wrote me a Letter purposely to draw from me my Sentiments in Writing on the then State of Affairs. I wrote a pretty free Answer, which I know was immediately communicated and a good deal handed about among them. For your *private Amusement* I send you Copies. I wish you may be able to read them, as they are very badly written by a very blundering Clerk.

TO JOSEPH PRIESTLEY

Dear Sir, London, Sept. 19, 1772

In the Affair of so much Importance to you, wherein you ask my Advice, I cannot for want of sufficient Premises, advise you *what* to determine, but if you please I will tell you *how*. When these difficult Cases occur, they are difficult chiefly because while we have them under Consideration all the Reasons *pro* and *con* are not present to the Mind at the same time; but sometimes one Set present themselves, and at other times another, the first being out of Sight. Hence the various Purposes or Inclinations that alternately prevail, and the Uncertainty that perplexes us. To get over this, my Way is, to divide half a Sheet of Paper by a Line into two Columns, writing over the one *Pro*, and over the other *Con*. Then during three or four Days Consideration I put down under the different Heads short Hints of the different Motives that at different Times occur to me for or against the Measure. When I have thus got them all together in one View, I endeavour to estimate their respective Weights; and where I find two, one on each side, that seem equal, I strike them both out: If I find a Reason *pro* equal to some two Reasons *con*, I strike out the three. If I judge some two Reasons *con* equal to some three Reasons *pro*, I strike out the five; and thus proceeding I find at length where the Ballance lies; and if after a Day or two of farther Consideration nothing new that is of Importance occurs on either side, I come to a Determination accordingly. And tho' the Weight of Reasons cannot be taken with the Precision of Algebraic Quantities, yet when each is thus considered separately and comparatively, and the whole lies before me, I think I can judge better, and am less likely to make a rash Step; and in fact I have found great Advantage from this kind of Equation, in what may be called *Moral* or *Prudential Algebra*. Wishing sincerely that you may determine for the best, I am ever, my dear Friend, Yours most affectionately

TO WILLIAM STRAHAN

Mr. Strahan,   Philadelphia, July 5, 1775

You are a Member of Parliament, and one of that Majority which has doomed my Country to Destruction. You have begun to burn our Towns, and murder our People. Look upon your Hands! They are stained with the Blood of your Relations! You and I were long Friends: You are now my Enemy, and I am, Yours,

TO DAVID HARTLEY

Philadelphia, Oct. 3, 1775

I wish as ardently as you can do for peace, and should rejoice exceedingly in co-operating with you to that end. But every ship from Britain brings some intelligence of new measures that tend more and more to exasperate; and it seems to me that until you have found by dear experience the reducing us by force impracticable, you will think of nothing fair and reasonable.—We have as yet resolved only on defensive measures. If you would recall your forces and stay at home, we should meditate nothing to injure you. A little time so given for cooling on both sides would have excellent effects. But you will goad and provoke us. You despise us too much; and you are insensible of the Italian adage, that *there is no little enemy.*—I am persuaded the body of the British people are our friends; but they are changeable, and by your lying Gazettes may soon be made our enemies. Our respect for them will proportionally diminish; and I see clearly we are on the high road to mutual enmity, hatred, and detestation. A separation will of course be inevitable.— 'Tis a million of pities so fair a plan as we have hitherto been engaged in for increasing strength and empire with *public felicity*, should be destroyed by the mangling hands of a few blundering ministers. It will not be destroyed: God will protect and prosper it: You will only exclude yourselves from any share in it.—We hear that more ships and troops are coming out. We know you may do us a great deal of mischief, but we are determined to bear it patiently as long as we can; but if you flatter yourselves with beating us into submission, you know neither the people nor the *country.*

The congress is still sitting, and will wait the result of their *last* petition.

TO LORD HOWE

My Lord,

I received, safe, the Letters your Lordship so kindly forwarded to me, and beg you to accept my Thanks.

The Official Dispatches to which you refer me, contain nothing more than what we bad seen in the Act of Parliament, viz. Offers of Pardon upon Submission; which I was sorry to find, as it must give your Lordship Pain to be sent so far on so hopeless a Business.

Directing Pardons to be offered to the Colonies, who are the very Parties injured, expresses indeed that Opinion of our Ignorance, Baseness, and Insensibility, which your uninform'd and proud Nation has long been pleased to entertain of us; but it can nave no other Effect than that of increasing our Resentments.—It is impossible we should think of Submission to a Government, that has with the most wanton Barbarity and Cruelty, burned our defenceless Towns in the midst of Winter, excited the Savages to massacre our Farmers, and our Slaves to murder their Masters, and is even now bringing foreign Mercenaries to deluge our Settlements with Blood. These atrocious Injuries have extinguished every remaining Spark of Affection for that Parent Country we once held so dear: But were it possible for *us* to forget and forgive them, it is not possible for *you* (I mean the British Nation) to forgive the People you have so heavily injured; you can never confide again in those as Fellow Subjects, and permit them to enjoy equal Freedom, to whom you know you have given such just Cause of lasting Enmity. And this must impel you, were we again under your Government, to endeavour the breaking our Spirit by the severest Tyranny, and obstructing by every means in your Power our growing Strength and Prosperity.

But your Lordship mentions "the Kings paternal Solicitude for promoting the Establishment of lasting *Peace* and Union with the Colonies." If by *Peace* is here meant, a Peace to be entered into between Britain and America as distinct States now at War, and his Majesty has given your Lordship Powers to treat with us of such a Peace, I may venture to say, tho' without Authority, that I think a Treaty for that purpose not yet quite impracticable, before we enter into Foreign Alliances. But I am persuaded you have no such Powers. Your Nation, tho' by punishing those American Governors who have created and fomented the Discord, rebuilding our burnt Towns, and repairing as far as possible the Mischiefs done us, She might Recover a great Share of our Regard and the greatest part of our growing Commerce, with all the Advantages of that additional Strength to be derived from a Friendship with us; I know too well her abounding Pride and deficient Wisdom, to believe she will ever take such Salutary Measures. Her Fondness for Conquest as a Warlike Nation; her Lust of Dominion as an Ambitious one; and her Thirst for a gainful Monopoly as a Commercial one (none of them legitimate Causes of War) will all join to hide from her Eyes every View of her true Interests; and continually goad her on in these ruinous distant Expeditions, so destructive both of Lives and of Treasure, that they must prove as pernicious to her in the End as the Croisades formerly were to most of the Nations of Europe.

I have not the Vanity, my Lord, to think of intimidating by thus predicting the Effects of this War; for I know it will in England have the Fate of all my former Predictions, not to be believed till the Event shall verify it.

Long did I endeavour with unfeigned and unwearied Zeal, to preserve from breaking, that fine and noble China Vase the British Empire: for I knew that being once broken, the separate Parts could not retain even their Share of the Strength or Value that existed in the Whole, and that a perfect Re-Union of those Parts could scarce ever be hoped for. Your Lordship may possibly remember the Tears of Joy that wet my Cheek, when, at your good Sister's in London, you once gave me Expectations that a Reconciliation might soon take place. I had the Misfortune to find those Expectations disappointed, and to be treated as the Cause of the Mischief I was labouring to prevent. My Consolation under that groundless and malevolent Treatment was, that I retained the Friendship of many Wise and Good Men in that Country, and among the rest, some Share in the Regard of Lord Howe.

The well founded Esteem, and permit me to say Affection, which I shall always have for your Lordship, makes it painful to me to see you engag'd in conducting a War, the great Ground of which, as expressed in your Letter, is "the Necessity of preventing the American Trade from passing into foreign Channels." To me it seems, that neither the obtaining or retaining any Trade, how valuable soever, is an Object for which Men may justly Spill each others Blood; that the true and sure means of extending and securing Commerce is the goodness and cheapness of Commodities; and that the profits of no Trade can ever be equal to the Expense of compelling it, and of holding it, by Fleets and Armies. I consider this War against us, therefore, as both unjust and unwise; and I am persuaded cool and dispassionate Posterity will condemn to Infamy those who advised it; and that even Success will not save from some degree of Dishonour, those who voluntarily engag'd to conduct it. I know your great Motive in coming hither was the Hope of being instrumental in a Reconciliation; and I believe when you find *that* impossible on any Terms given you to propose, you will relinquish so odious a Command, and return to a more honourable private Station. With the greatest and most sincere Respect I have the honour to be, My Lord your Lordships most obedient humble Servant

TO RICHARD PRICE

Dear Sir,   Passy, Oct. 9, 1780

Besides the Pleasure of their Company, I had the great Satisfaction of hearing by your two valuable Friends, and learning from your Letter, that you enjoy a good State of Health. May God continue it, as well for the Good of Mankind as for your Comfort. I thank you much for the second Edition of your excellent Pamphlet: I forwarded that you sent to Mr. Dana, he being in Holland. I wish also to see the Piece you have written (as Mr. Jones tells me) on Toleration. I do not expect that your new Parliament will be either wiser or honester than the last. All Projects to procure an honest one, by Place Bills, &c., appear to me vain and Impracticable. The true Cure, I imagine, is to be found only in rendring all Places unprofitable, and the King too poor to give Bribes and Pensions. Till this is done, which can only be by a Revolution (and I think you have not Virtue enough left to procure one), your Nation will always be plundered, and obliged to pay by Taxes the Plunderers for Plundering and Ruining. Liberty and Virtue therefore join in the call, COME OUT OF HER, MY PEOPLE!

I am fully of your Opinion respecting religious Tests; but tho' the People of Massachusetts have not in their new Constitution kept quite clear of them, yet, if we consider what that People were 100 Years ago, we must allow they have gone great Lengths in Liberality of Sentiment on religious Subjects; and we may hope for greater Degrees of Perfection, when their Constitution, some years hence, shall be revised. If Christian Preachers had continued to teach as Christ and his Apostles did, without Salaries, and as the Quakers now do, I imagine Tests would never have existed; for I think they were invented, not so much to secure Religion itself, as the Emoluments of it. When a Religion is good, I conceive that it will support itself; and when it cannot support itself, and God does not take care to support it, so that its Professors are oblig'd to call for the help of the Civil Power, 'tis a sign, I apprehend, of its being a bad one. But I shall be out of my Depth, if I wade any deeper in Theology, and I will not trouble you with Politicks, nor with News which are almost as uncertain; but conclude with a heartfelt Wish to embrace you once more, and enjoy your sweet Society in Peace, among our honest, worthy, ingenious Friends at the *London.* Adieu,

TO MARY HEWSON

PASSY, JAN. 27, 1783

—The Departure of my dearest Friend, which I learn from your last Letter, greatly affects me. To meet with her once more in this Life was one of the principal Motives of my proposing to visit England again, before my Return to America. The last Year carried off my Friends Dr. Pringle, and Dr. Fothergill, Lord Kaims, and Lord le Despencer. This has begun to take away the rest, and strikes the hardest. Thus the Ties I had to that Country, and indeed to the World in general, are loosened one by one, and I shall soon have no Attachment left to make me unwilling to follow.

I intended writing when I sent the 11 Books, but I lost the Time in looking for the 12th. I wrote with that; and hope it came to hand. I therein ask'd your Counsel about my coming to England. On Reflection, I think I can, from my Knowledge of your Prudence, foresee what it will be, viz. not to come too soon, lest it should seem braving and insulting some who ought to be respected. I shall, therefore, omit that Journey till I am near going to America, and then just step over to take Leave of my Friends, and spend a few days with you. I purpose bringing Ben with me, and perhaps may leave him under your Care.

At length we are in Peace, God be praised, and long, very long, may it continue. All Wars are Follies, very expensive, and very mischievous ones. When will Mankind be convinced of this, and agree to settle their Differences by Arbitration? Were they to do it, even by the Cast of a Dye, it would be better than by Fighting and destroying each other.

Spring is coming on, when Travelling will be delightful. Can you not, when your children are all at School, make a little Party, and take a Trip hither? I have now a large House, delightfully situated, in which I could accommodate you and two or three Friends, and I am but half an Hour's Drive from Paris.

In looking forward, Twenty-five Years seem a long Period, but, in looking back, how short! Could you imagine, that 'tis now full a Quarter of a Century since we were first acquainted? It was in 1757. During the greatest Part of the Time, I lived in the same House with my dear deceased Friend, your Mother; of course you and I saw and convers'd with each other much and often. It is to all our Honours, that in all that time we never had among us the smallest Misunderstanding. Our Friendship has been all clear Sunshine, without the least Cloud in its Hemisphere. Let me conclude by saying to you, what I have had too frequent Occasions to say to my other remaining old Friends, "The fewer we become, the more let us love one another." Adieu, and believe me ever yours most affectionately,

SIR JOSEPH BANKS

Dear Sir, Passy, July 27, 1783

I received your very kind letter by Dr. Blagden, and esteem myself much honoured by your friendly Remembrance. I have been too much and too closely engaged in public Affairs, since his being here, to enjoy all the Benefit of his Conversation you were so good as to intend me. I hope soon to have more Leisure, and to spend a part of it in those Studies, that are much more agreable to me than political Operations.

I join with you most cordially in rejoicing at the return of Peace. I hope it will be lasting, and that Mankind will at length, as they call themselves reasonable Creatures, have Reason and Sense enough to settle their Differences without cutting Throats; for, in my opinion, *there never was a good War, or a bad Peace.* What vast additions to the Conveniences and Comforts of Living might Mankind have acquired, if the Money spent in Wars had been employed in Works of public utility! What an extention of Agriculture even to the Tops of our Mountains; what Rivers rendered navigable, or joined by Canals; what Bridges, Acqueducts, new Roads, and other public Works, Edifices, and Improvements, rendering England a compleat Paradise, might not have been obtain'd by spending those Millions in doing good, which in the last War have been spent in doing Mischief; in bringing Misery into thousands of Families, and destroying the Lives of so many thousands of working people who might have perform'd the useful labour!

I am pleased with the late astronomical Discoveries made by our Society. Furnished as all Europe now is with Academies of Science, with nice Instruments and the Spirit of Experiment, the progress of human knowledge will be rapid, and discoveries made, of which we have at present no Conception. I begin to be almost sorry I was born so soon, since I cannot have the happiness of knowing what will be known 100 years hence.

I wish continued success to the Labours of the Royal Society, and that you may long adorn their chair; being, with the highest esteem, dear Sir, &c.

P.S. Dr. Blagden will acquaint you with the experiment of a vast Globe sent up into the Air, much talked of here, and which, if prosecuted, may furnish means of new knowledge.

TO GEORGE WHATLEY

Dear Old Friend,   Passy, May 23, 1785

... I have some reason to wish, that, in a future State, I may not only be *as well as I was*, but a little better. And I hope it; for I, too, with your Poet, *trust in God*. And when I observe, that there is great Frugality, as well as Wisdom, in his Works, since he has evidently been sparing both of Labour and Materials; for by various wonderful Inventions of Propagation, he has provided for the continual peopling his World with Plants and Animals, without being at the trouble of repeated new Creations; and by the natural Reduction of compound Substances to their original Elements, capable of being employ'd in new Compositions, he has prevented the Necessity of creating new Matter; so that the Earth, Water, Air, and perhaps Fire, which being compounded form Wood, do, when the Wood is dissolved, return, and again become Air, Earth, Fire, and Water; I say that when I see nothing annihilated, not even a Drop of Water Wasted, I cannot suspect the Annihilation of Souls, or believe that he will suffer the daily Waste of Millions of Minds ready made that now exist, and put himself to the continual trouble of making new ones. Thus finding myself to exist in the World, I believe I shall, in some Shape or other, always exist; and, with all the inconveniences human Life is liable to, I shall not object to a new Edition of mine; hoping, however, that the Errata of the last may be corrected.

THE
MAXIMS
OF
POOR
RICHARD

INTRODUCTION

"I might in this place attempt to gain thy Favour, by declaring that I write Almanacks with no other view than that of the publick Good; but in this I should not be sincere; and Men are now a-days too wise to be deceiv'd by Pretences how specious soever. The plain Truth of the Matter is, I am excessive poor, and my Wife, good Woman, is, I tell her, excessive proud; she cannot bear, she says, to sit spinning in her Shift of Tow, while I do nothing but gaze at the Stars; and has threatned more than once to burn all my Books and Rattling-Traps (as she calls my Instruments) if I do not make some profitable Use of them for the good of my Family. The printer has offer'd me some considerable share of the Profits, and I have thus begun to comply with my Dame's desire."

So begins the first installment of *Poor Richard's Almanack*, one of the most famous of all Benjamin Franklin's literary inventions. Published in December of 1732, it inaugurated an annual pamphlet series that ran for twenty-six installments until it was discontinued in 1758. Franklin presented it as the work of Richard Saunders, a stargazing scholar goaded by his long-suffering wife Bridget to put his book-learning to practical use in support of their household. Bridget's advice certainly proved sound: the almanack—whose true authorship was never in question to the overwhelming majority of its readers—sold upwards of 10,000 copies annually, making it not only one of Franklin's most popular publications, but among his most profitable.

Franklin modeled his almanack on traditional almanacks, which for centuries had been popular sources of news, weather forecasts, discussions of astronomical phenomena, household hints, games and puzzles, and entertainments. Influenced by Jonathan Swift and other satirists, Franklin also brought a good deal of humor to his almanack, using it to lampoon some of the more peculiar uses people turned to such books for. The first installment was one of several in which Richard used his supposedly superior astrological skills to predict the impending death date of a fellow astrologer (which, of course, did not prove accurate). Such whimsically spurious predictions became a strong selling point for the almanack. In 1748, in gratitude to his supportive public, Richard offered a supposedly revamped version of his almanack, *Poor Richard Improved*. It continued under this title for another ten installments.

In addition to topical news and advice, Franklin filled out each installment of the almanack with witty maxims and aphorisms. These usually appeared in a list at the end of the pamphlet, but sometimes were interspersed with the poetry, obituaries, scientific information, celestial observations, and farming tips that made up the bulk of each installment. In only a few instances, the maxims represented the entirety of the pamphlet. Some of the maxims are genuine folk wisdom that had been part of the oral tradition for centuries, while others were borrowed from historical sources. It was Franklin's idea to collect them as witty expressions of common sense, and they remain one of his most enduring contributions to early American literature. The following selection reproduces most of the maxims of Poor Richard as they were published in annual installments of the almanack.

Never spare the Parson's wine, nor the Baker's pudding.

> Visits should be short, like a winters day,
> Lest you're too troublesom hasten away.

A house without woman & Fire-light, is like a body without soul or sprite.

Kings & Bears often worry their keepers.

Light purse, heavy heart.

He's a Fool that makes his Doctor his Heir.

Ne'er take a wife till thou hast a house (& a fire) to put her in.

He's gone, and forgot nothing but to say *Farewel*—to his creditors.

Love well, whip well.

> Let my respected friend *J. G.*
> Accept this humble verse of me. *viz.*
> Ingenious, learned, envy'd Youth,
> Go on as thou'st began;
> Even thy enemies take pride
> That thou'rt their countryman.

Hunger never saw bad bread.

Beware of meat twice boil'd, & an old foe reconcil'd.

Great Talkers, little Doers.

A rich rogue, is like a fat hog, who never does good til as dead as a log.

Relation without friendship, friendship without power, power without will, will witho. effect, effect without profit, & profit without virtue, are not worth a farto.

Eat to live, and not live to eat.

> March windy, and April rainy,
> makes *May* the pleasantest month of any.

The favour of the Great is no inheritance.

Fools make feasts and wise men eat 'em.

Beware of the young Doctor & the old Barber.

He has chang'd his one ey'd horse for a blind one.

The poor have little, beggars none, the rich too much, *enough* not one.

After 3 days men grow weary, of a wench, a guest, & weather rainy.

To lengthen thy Life, lessen thy Meals.

The proof of gold is fire, the proof of woman, gold; the proof of man, a woman.

After feasts made, the maker scratches his head.

Neither Shame nor Grace yet *Bob*.

Many estates are spent in the getting,
    Since women for tea forsook spinning & knitting.

He that lies down with Dogs, shall rise up with fleas.

A fat kitchin, a lean Will.

Distrust & caution are the parents of security.

Tongue double, brings trouble.

Take counsel in wine, but resolve afterwards in water.

He that drinks fast, pays slow.

Great famine when wolves eat wolves.

A good Wife lost is God's gift lost.

A taught horse, and a woman to teach, and teachers practising what they preach.

He is ill cloth'd, who is bare of Virtue.

The heart of a fool is in his mouth, but the mouth of a wise man is in his heart.

Men & Melons are hard to know.

He's the best physician that knows the worthlessness of the most medicines.

A fine genius in his own country, is like gold in the mine.

There is no little enemy.

He has lost his Boots but sav'd his spurs.

The old Man has given all to his Son: O fool! to undress thy self before thou art going to bed.

Cheese and salt meat, should be sparingly eat.

Doors and walls are fools paper.

Anoint a villain and he'll stab you, stab him & he'll anoint you.

Keep your mouth wet, feet dry.

Where bread is wanting, all's to be sold.

There is neither honour nor gain, got in dealing with a vil-lain.

> The fool hath made a vow, I guess,
> Never to let the Fire have peace.

Snowy winter, a plentiful harvest.

Nothing more like a Fool, than a drunken Man.

> God works wonders now & then;
> Behold! a Lawyer, an honest Man!

He that lives carnally, won't live eternally.

Innocence is its own Defence.

> Time *eateth* all things, could old Poets say;
> The Times are chang'd, our times *drink* all away.

Never mind it, she'l be sober after the Holidays.

Would you live with ease,
Do what you ought, and not what you please.

Better slip with foot than tongue.

You cannot pluck roses without fear of thorns,
Nor enjoy a fair wife without danger of horns.

Without justice, courage is weak.

Many dishes many diseases,
Many medicines few cures.

Where carcasses are, eagles will gather,
And where good laws are, much people flock thither.

Hot things, sharp things, sweet things, cold things
All rot the teeth, and make them look like old things.

Blame-all and *Praise-all* are two blockheads.

Be temperate in wine, in eating, girls, & sloth;
Or the Gout will seize you and plague you both.

No man e'er was glorious, who was not laborious.

What pains our Justice takes his faults to hide,
With half that pains sure he might cure 'em quite.

In success be moderate.

Take this remark from *Richard* poor and lame,
Whate'er's begun in anger ends in shame.

What one relishes, nourishes.

Fools multiply folly.

Beauty & folly are old companions.

Hope of gain
Lessens pain.

All things are easy to Industry,
All things difficult to *Sloth*.

If you ride a Horse, sit close and tight,
If you ride a Man, sit easy and light.

A new truth is a truth, an old error is an error,
Tho' *Clodpate* wont allow either.

Don't think to hunt two hares with one dog.

Astrologers say,
This is a good Day,
To make Love in May.

Who pleasure gives,
Shall joy receive.

Be not sick too late, nor well too soon.

Where there's Marriage without Love, there will be Love without Marriage.

Lawyers, Preachers, and Tomtits Eggs, there are more of them hatch'd than come to perfection.

Be neither silly, nor cunning, but wise.

Neither a Fortress nor a Maidenhead will hold out long after they begin to parly.

Jack *Little* sow'd little, & little he'll reap.

All things are cheap to the saving, dear to the wasteful.

Would you persuade, speak of Interest, not of Reason.

> Some men grow mad by studying much to know,
> But who grows mad by studying good to grow.

Happy's the Woing, that's not long a doing.

Don't value a man for the Quality he is of, but for the Qualities he possesses.

Bucephalus the Horse of *Alexand* hath as lasting fame as his Master.

> Rain or Snow,
> To *Chili* go,
> You'll find it so,
> For ought we know.
> Time will show.

There have been as great Souls unknown to fame as any of the most famous.

Do good to thy Friend to keep him, to thy enemy to gain him.

A good Man is seldom uneasy, an ill one never easie.

Teach your child to hold his tongue, he'll learn fast enough to speak.

He that cannot obey, cannot command.

An innocent *Plowman* is more worthy than a vicious *Prince*.

Sam's Religion is like a *Chedder Cheese*, 'tis made of the *milk* of one & twenty Parishes.

> Grief for a dead Wife, & a troublesome Guest,
> Continues to the *threshold*, and there is at rest;
> But I mean such wives as are none of the best.

As Charms are nonsence, Nonsence is a Charm.

An Egg to day is better than a Hen to-morrow.

Drink Water, Put the Money in your Pocket, and leave the *Dry-bellyach* in the *Punchbowl*.

He that is rich need not live sparingly, and he that can live sparingly need not be rich.

If you wou'd be reveng'd of your enemy, govern your self.

A wicked Hero will turn his back to an innocent coward.

> *Laws* like to *Cobwebs* catch small Flies,
> Great ones break thro' before your eyes.

Strange, that he who lives by Shifts, can seldom shift himself.

As sore places meet most rubs, proud folks meet most affronts.

The magistrate should obey the Laws, the People should obey the magistrate.

When 'tis fair be sure take your Great coat with you.

He does not possess Wealth, it possesses him.

Necessity has no Law; I know some Attorneys of the name.

Onions can make ev'n Heirs and Widows weep.

Avarice and Happiness never saw each other, how then shou'd they become acquainted.

> The thrifty maxim of the wary *Dutch*,
> Is to save all the Money they can touch.

He that waits upon Fortune, is never sure of a Dinner.

A learned blockhead is a greater blockhead than an ignorant one.

Marry your Son when you will, but your Daughter when you can.

1735

Look before, or you'll find yourself behind.

> Bad Commentators spoil the best of books,
> So God sends meat (they say) the devil Cooks.

Approve not of him who commends all you say.

By diligence and patience, the mouse bit in two the cable.

Full of courtesie, full of craft.

A little House well fill'd, a little Field well till'd, and a little Wife well will'd, are great Riches.

Old Maids lead Apes there, where the old Batchelors are turn'd to Apes.

Some are weatherwise, some are otherwise.

The poor man must walk to get meat for his stomach, the rich man to get a stomach to his meat.

He that goes far to marry, will either deceive or be deceived.

> Eyes and Priests
> Bear no Jests.

The Family of Fools is ancient.

Necessity never made a good bargain.

If Pride leads the Van, Beggary brings up the Rear.

There's many witty men whose brains can't fill their bellies.

Weighty Questions ask for deliberate Answers.

When ♂ and ♀ in ♂ lie,
Then, Maids, whate'er is ask'd of you, deny.

Be slow in chusing a Friend, slower in changing.

Old *Hob* was lately married in the Night,
What needed Day, his fair young Wife is light.

Pain wastes the Body, Pleasures the Understanding.

The cunning man steals a horse, the wise man lets him alone.

Nothing but Money,
Is sweeter than Honey.

Humility makes great men twice honourable.

A Ship under sail and a big-bellied Woman,
Are the handsomest two things that can be seen common.

Keep thy shop, & thy shop will keep thee.

The King's cheese is half wasted in parings: But no matter, 'tis made of the peoples milk.

What's given shines,
What's receiv'd is rusty.

Sloth and Silence are a Fool's Virtues.

Of learned Fools I have seen ten times ten,
Of unlearned wise men I have seen a hundred.

Three may keep a Secret, if two of them are dead.

Poverty wants some things, Luxury many things, Avarice all things.

A Lie stands on 1 leg, Truth on 2.

There's small Revenge in Words, but Words may be greatly revenged.

Great wits jump (says the Poet) and hit his Head against the Post.

A man is never so ridiculous by those Qualities that are his own as by those that he affects to have.

Deny Self for Self's sake.

> *Tim* moderate fare and abstinence much prizes,
> In publick, but in private gormandizes.

Ever since Follies have pleas'd, Fools have been able to divert.

It is better to take many Injuries than to give one.

Opportunity is the great Bawd.

Early to bed and early to rise, makes a man healthy wealthy and wise.

To be humble to Superiors is Duty, to Equals Courtesy, to Inferiors Nobleness.

Here comes the Orator! with his Flood of Words, and his Drop of Reason.

An old young man, will be a young old man.

Sal laughs at every thing you say. Why? Because she has fine Teeth.

> If what most men admire, they would despise,
> 'Twould look as if mankind were growing wise.

The Sun never repents of the good he does, nor does he ever demand a recompence.

Are you angry that others disappoint you? remember you cannot depend upon yourself.

One Mend-fault is worth two Findfaults, but one Findfault is better than two Makefaults.

> *Reader*, I wish thee Health, Wealth, Happiness,
> And may kind Heaven thy Year's Industry bless.

1736

He is no clown that drives the plow, but he that doth clownish things.

If you know how to spend less than you get, you have the Philosophers-Stone.

The good Paymaster is Lord of another man's Purse.

Fish & Visitors stink in 3 days.

He that has neither fools, whores nor beggars among his kindred, is the son of a thunder-gust.

Diligence is the Mother of Good-Luck.

He that lives upon Hope, dies farting.

Do not do that which you would not have known.

Never praise your Cyder, Horse, or Bedfellow.

Wealth is not his that has it, but his that enjoys it.

Tis easy to see, hard to foresee.

In a discreet man's mouth, a publick thing is private.

Let thy maidservant be faithful, strong, and homely.

Keep flax from fire, youth from gaming.

Bargaining has neither friends nor relations.

Admiration is the Daughter of Ignorance.

There's more old Drunkards than old Doctors.

She that paints her Face, thinks of her Tail.

Here comes Courage! that seiz'd the lion absent, and run away from the present mouse.

He that takes a wife, takes care.

Nor Eye in a letter, nor Hand in a purse, nor Ear in the secret of another.

He that buys by the penny, maintains not only himself, but other people.

He that can have Patience, can have what he will.

Now I've a sheep and a cow, every body bids me good morrow.

God helps them that help themselves.

Why does the blind man's wife paint herself.

None preaches better than the ant, and she says nothing.

The absent are never without fault, nor the present without excuse.

Gifts burst rocks.

> If wind blows on you thro' a hole,
> Make your will and take care of your soul.

The rotten Apple spoils his Companion.

He that sells upon trust, loses many friends, and always wants money.

Don't throw stones at your neighbours, if your own windows are glass.

The excellency of hogs is fatness, of men virtue.

Good wives and good plantations are made by good husbands.

Pox take you, is no curse to some people.

Force shites upon Reason's Back.

Lovers, Travellers, and Poets, will give money to be heard.

He that speaks much, is much mistaken.

Creditors have better memories than debtors.

Forwarn'd, forearm'd, unless in the case of Cuckolds, who are often
forearm'd before warn'd.

Three things are men most liable to be cheated in, a Horse, a Wig, and
a Wife.

He that lives well, is learned enough.

Poverty, Poetry, and new Titles of Honour, make Men ridiculous.

He that scatters Thorns, let him not go barefoot.

There's none deceived but he that trusts.

God heals, and the Doctor takes the Fees.

If you desire many things, many things will seem but a few.

Mary's mouth costs her nothing, for she never opens it but at others expence.

Receive before you write, but write before you pay.

I saw few die of Hunger, of Eating 100000.

Maids of *America*, who gave you bad teeth?
   Answ. Hot Soupings & frozen Apples.

Marry your Daughter and eat fresh Fish betimes.

If God blesses a Man, his Bitch brings forth Pigs.

He that would live in peace & at ease,

Must not speak all he knows, nor judge all he sees.

1737

The greatest monarch on the proudest throne, is oblig'd to sit upon his own arse.

The Master-piece of Man, is to live to the purpose.

He that steals the old man's supper, do's him no wrong.

A countryman between 2 Lawyers, is like a fish between two cats.

He that can take rest is greater than he that can take cities.

The misers cheese is wholesomest.

Love & lordship hate companions.

The nearest way to come at glory, is to do that for conscience which we do for glory.

There is much money given to be laught at, though the purchasers don't know it; witness *A's* fine horse, & *B's* fine house.

He that can compose himself, is wiser than he that composes books.

Poor Dick, eats like a well man, and drinks like a sick.

After crosses and losses men grow humbler & wiser.

Love, Cough, & a Smoke, can't well be hid.

Well done is better than well said.

> Fine linnen, girls and gold so bright,
> Chuse not to take by candle-light.

He that can travel well afoot, keeps a good horse.

There are no ugly Loves, nor handsome Prisons.

No better relation than a prudent & faithful Friend.

A Traveller should have a hog's nose, deer's legs, and an ass's back.

At the working man's house hunger looks in but dares not enter.

A good Lawyer a bad Neighbour.

> Certainlie these things agree,
> The Priest, the Lawyer, & Death all three:
> Death takes both the weak and the strong.
> The lawyer takes from both right and wrong,
> And the priest from living and dead has his Fee.

The worst wheel of the cart makes the most noise.

Don't misinform your Doctor nor your Lawyer.

> I never saw an oft-transplanted tree,
> Nor yet an oft-removed family,
> That throve so well as those that settled be.

Let the Letter stay for the Post, and not the Post for the Letter.

Three good meals a day is bad living.

Tis better leave for an enemy at one's death, than beg of a friend in one's life.

> To whom thy secret thou dost tell,
> To him thy freedom thou dost sell.

If you'd have a Servant that you like, serve your self.

He that pursues two Hares at once, does not catch one and lets t'other go.

If you want a neat wife, chuse her on a Saturday.

If you have time dont wait for time.

Tell a miser he's rich, and a woman she's old, you'll get no money of one, nor kindness of t'other.

Don't go to the doctor with every distemper, nor to the lawyer with every quarrel, nor to the pot for every thirst.

The Creditors are a superstitious sect, great observers of set days and times.

The noblest question in the world is *What Good may I do in it?*

Nothing so popular as GOODNESS.

There are three faithful friends, an old wife, an old dog, and ready money.

Great talkers should be cropt, for they've no need of ears.

If you'd have your shoes last, put no nails in 'em.

Who has deceiv'd thee so oft as thy self?

Is there any thing Men take more pains about than to render themselves
unhappy?

Nothing brings more pain than too much pleasure; nothing more bondage
than too much liberty, (or libertinism.)

Read much, but not many Books.

He that would have a short Lent, let him borrow Money to be repaid
at Easter.

Write with the learned, pronounce with the vulgar.

Fly Pleasures, and they'll follow you.

Squirrel-like she covers her back with her tail.

Cæsar did not merit the triumphal Car, more than he that conquers himself.

Hast thou virtue? acquire also the graces & beauties of virtue.

Buy what thou hast no need of; and e'er long thou shalt sell thy necessaries.

If thou hast wit & learning, add to it Wisdom and Modesty.

You may be more happy than Princes, if you will be more virtuous.

> If you wou'd not be forgotten
> As soon as you are dead and rotten,
> Either write things worth reading,
> or do things worth the writing.

Sell not virtue to purchase wealth, nor Liberty to purchase power.

God bless the King, and grant him long to Reign.

Let thy vices die before thee.

Keep your eyes wide open before marriage, half shut afterwards.

The ancients tell us what is best; but we must learn of the moderns what is fittest.

Since I cannot govern my own tongue, tho' within my own teeth, how can I hope to govern the tongues of others?

Tis less discredit to abridge petty charges, than to stoop to petty Gettings.

Since thou art not sure of a minute, throw not away an hour.

If you do what you should not, you must hear what you would not.

Defer not thy well-doing; be not like St. *George*, who is always a horseback, and never rides on.

Wish not so much to live long as to live well.

As we must account for every idle word, so we must for every idle silence.

I have never seen the Philosopher's Stone that turns lead into Gold, but I have known the pursuit of it turn a Man's Gold into Lead.

Never intreat a servant to dwell with thee.

Time is an herb that cures all Diseases.

Reading makes a full Man, Meditation a profound Man, discourse a clear Man.

If any man flatters me, I'll flatter him again; tho' he were my best Friend.

Wish a miser long life, and you wish him no good.

None but the well-bred man knows how to confess a fault, or acknowledge himself in an error.

Drive thy business; let not that drive thee.

There is much difference between imitating a good man, and counterfeiting him.

Wink at small faults; remember thou hast great ones.

Eat to please thyself, but dress to please others.

Search others for their virtues, thy self for thy vices.

> Each year one vicious habit rooted out,
> In time might make the worst Man good throughout.

When Death puts out our Flame, the Snuff will tell,
If we were Wax, or Tallow by the Smell.

At a great Pennyworth, pause a while.

As to his Wife, *John* minds St. *Paul*, He's one
That hath a Wife, and is as if he'd none.

Kings and Bears often worry their Keepers.

If thou wouldst live long, live well; for Folly and Wickedness shorten Life.

Prythee isn't Miss *Cloe's* a comical Case?
She lends out her Tail, and she borrows her Face.

Trust thy self, and another shall not betray thee.

He that pays for Work before it's done, has but a pennyworth for twopence.

Historians relate, not so much what is done, as what they would have believed.

O Maltster! break that cheating Peck; 'tis plain,
When e'er you use it, you're a Knave in Grain.

Doll learning *propria quæ maribus* without book,
Like *Nomen crescentis genitivo* doth look.

Grace thou thy House, and let not that grace thee.

Thou canst not joke an Enemy into a Friend; but thou may'st a Friend into
an Enemy.

Eyes & Priests
Bear no Jests.

He that falls in love with himself, will have no Rivals.

Let thy Child's first Lesson be Obedience, and the second may be what thou wilt.

Blessed is he that expects nothing, for he shall never be disappointed.

Rather go to bed supperless, than run in debt for a Breakfast.

Let thy Discontents be Secrets.

A Man of Knowledge like a rich Soil, feeds
If not a world of Corn, a world of Weeds.

A modern Wit is one of *David's* Fools.

No Resolution of Repenting hereafter, can be sincere.

Pollio, who values nothing that's within,
Buys Books as men hunt Beavers,—for their Skin.

Honour thy Father and Mother, *i.e.* Live so as to be an Honour to them tho' they are dead.

If thou injurest Conscience, it will have its Revenge on thee.

Hear no ill of a Friend, nor speak any of an Enemy.

Pay what you owe, and you'll know what's your own.

Be not niggardly of what costs thee nothing, as courtesy, counsel, & countenance.

Thirst after Desert, not Reward.

Beware of him that is slow to anger: He is angry for something, and will not be pleased for nothing.

No longer virtuous no longer free; is a Maxim as true with regard to a private Person as a Common-wealth.

> When Man and Woman die, as Poets sung,
> His Heart's the last part moves, her last, the tongue.

Proclaim not all thou knowest, all thou owest, all thou hast, nor all thou canst.

Let our Fathers and Grandfathers be valued for *their* Goodness, ourselves for our own.

Industry need not wish.

Sin is not hurtful because it is forbidden but it is forbidden because it's hurtful. Nor is a Duty beneficial because it is commanded, but it is commanded, because it's beneficial.

> *A* — , they say, has Wit; for what?
> For writing? — No; For writing not.

> *George* came to the Crown without striking a Blow.
> Ah! quoth the Pretender, would I could do so.

Love, and be lov'd.

O Lazy-Bones! Dost thou think God would have given thee Arms and Legs, if he had not design'd thou should'st use them.

1740

To bear other Peoples Afflictions, every one has Courage enough, and to spare.

> No wonder *Tom* grows fat, th' unwieldy Sinner,
> Makes his whole Life but one continual Dinner.

An empty Bag cannot stand upright.

Happy that nation, fortunate that age, whose history is not diverting.

> What is a butterfly? At best
> He's but a caterpiller drest.
> The gaudy Fop's his picture just.

None are deceived but they that confide.

> An open Foe may prove a curse;
> But a pretended friend is worse.

> A wolf eats sheep but now and then,
> Ten Thousands are devour'd by Men.

> Man's tongue is soft, and bone doth lack;
> Yet a stroke therewith may break a man's back.

Many a Meal is lost for want of meat.

> To all apparent Beauties blind
> Each Blemish strikes an envious Mind.

There are lazy Minds as well as lazy Bodies.

Tricks and Treachery are the Practice of Fools, that have not Wit enough to be honest.

Who says Jack is not generous? he is always fond of giving, and cares not for receiving. —What? Why; Advice.

> The Man who with undaunted toils,
> sails unknown seas to unknown soils,
> With various wonders feasts his Sight:
> What stranger wonders does he write?

Fear not Death; for the sooner we die, the longer shall we be immortal.

> Those who in quarrels interpose,
> Must often wipe a bloody nose.

Promises may get thee Friends, but Nonperformance will turn them into Enemies.

> In other men we faults can spy,
> And blame the mote that dims their eye;
> Each little speck and blemish find;
> To our own stronger errors blind.

When you speak to a man, look on his eyes; when he speaks to thee, look
on his mouth.

> *Jane*, why those tears? why droops your head?
> Is then your other husband dead?
> Or doth a worse disgrace betide?
> Hath no one since his death apply'd?

Observe all men; thy self most.

Thou haæter eat salt with the Philosophers of *Greece*, than sugar with the
Courtiers of *Italy*.

> Seek Virtue, and, of that possest,
> To Providence, resign the rest.

Marry above thy match, and thou'lt get a Master.

Fear to do ill, and you need fear nought else.

He makes a Foe who makes a jest.

> Can grave and formal pass for wise,
> When Men the solemn Owl despise?

Some are justly laught at for keeping their Money foolishly, others for
spending it idly: He is the greatest fool that lays it out in a purchase
of repentance.

> Who knows a fool, must know his brother;
> For one will recommend another.

Avoid dishonest Gain: No price;
Can recompence the Pangs of Vice.

When befriended, remember it:
When you befriend, forget it.

Great souls with gen'rous pity melt;
Which coward tyrants never felt.

Employ thy time well, if thou meanest to gain leisure.

A Flatterer never seems absurd:
The Flatter'd always take his Word.

Lend Money to an Enemy, and thou'lt gain him, to a Friend and thou'lt lose him.

Neither praise nor dispraise, till seven Christmasses be over.

1741

Enjoy the present hour, be mindful of the past;
And neither fear nor wish the Approaches of the last.

Best is the Tongue that feels the rein;—
He that talks much, must talk in vain;
We from the wordy Torrent fly:
Who listens to the chattering Pye?

Learn of the skilful: He that teaches himself, hath a fool for his master.

Think *Cato* sees thee.

No Wood without Bark.

> *Monkeys* warm with envious spite,
> Their most obliging Friends will bite;—
> And, fond to copy human Ways,
> Practise new Mischiefs all their days.

Joke went out, and brought home his fellow, and they two began a quarrel.

Let thy discontents be thy Secrets; — if the world knows them, 'twill despise *thee* and increase *them*.

> E'er you remark another's Sin,
> Bid your own Conscience look within.

Anger and Folly walk cheek-by-jole; Repentance treads on both their Heels.

Turn Turk *Tim*, and renounce thy Faith in Words as well as Actions: Is it worse to follow *Mahomet* than the Devil?

Don't overload Gratitude; if you do, she'll kick.

Be always asham'd to catch thy self idle.

> Where yet was ever found the Mother,
> Who'd change her booby for another?

At 20 years of age the Will reigns; at 30 the Wit; at 40 the Judgment.

Christianity commands us to pass by Injuries; Policy, to let them pass by us.

Lying rides upon Debt's back.

They who have nothing to be troubled at, will be troubled at nothing.

> Wife from thy Spouse each blemish hide
> More than from all the World beside:
> Let DECENCY be all thy Pride.

Nick's Passions grow fat and hearty; his Understanding looks consumptive!

> If evils come not, then our fears are vain:
> And if they do, Fear but augments the pain.

If you would keep your Secret from an enemy, tell it not to a friend.

Rob not for burnt offerings.

> *Bess* brags she 'as *Beauty*, and can prove the same;
> As how? why thus, Sir, 'tis her *puppy's* name.

Up, Sluggard, and waste not life; in the grave will be sleeping enough.

Well done, is twice done.

Clearly spoken, Mr. Fog! You explain English by Greek.

Formio bewails his Sins with the same heart,
As Friends do Friends when they're about to part.
Believe it *Formio* will not entertain,
One chearful Thought till they do meet again.

Honours change Manners.

Jack eating rotten cheese, did say,
Like *Sampson* I my thousands slay;
I vow, quoth *Roger*, so you do,
And with the self-same weapon too.

There are no fools so troublesome as those that have wit.

Quarrels never could last long,
If on one side only lay the wrong.

Let no Pleasure tempt thee, no Profit allure thee, no Ambition corrupt thee, no Example sway thee, no Persuasion move thee, to do any thing which thou knowest to be Evil; So shalt thou always live jollily: for a good Conscience is a continual Christmass.

1742

Strange! that a Man who has wit enough to write a Satyr; should have folly enough to publish it.

He that hath a Trade, hath an Estate.

Have you somewhat to do to-morrow; do it to-day.

> No workman without tools,
> Nor Lawyer without Fools,
> Can live by their Rules.

> The painful Preacher, like a candle bright,
> Consumes himself in giving others Light.

Speak and speed: the close mouth catches no flies.

Visit your Aunt, but not every Day; and call at your Brother's, but not every night.

Money and good Manners make the Gentleman.

Late Children, early Orphans.

> *Ben* beats his Pate, and fancys wit will come;
> But he may knock, there's no body at home.

The good Spinner hath a large Shift.

> *Tom*, vain's your Pains; They all will fail:
> Ne'er was good Arrow made of a Sow's Tail.

> Empty Free-booters, cover'd with Scorn:
> They went out for Wealth, & come ragged and torn,
> As the Ram went for Wool, and was sent back shorn.

Ill Customs & bad Advice are seldom forgotten.

He that sows thorns, should not go barefoot.

Men meet, mountains never.

When Knaves fall out, honest Men get their goods: When Priests dispute, we come at the Truth.

> *Kate* would have *Thomas*, no one blame her can:
> *Tom* won't have *Kate*, and who can blame the Man?

A large train makes a light Purse.

Death takes no bribes.

One good Husband is worth two good Wives; for the scarcer things are the more they're valued.

He that riseth late, must trot all day, and shall scarce overtake his business at night.

He that speaks ill of the Mare, will buy her.

You may drive a gift without a gimblet.

Eat few Suppers, and you'll need few Medicines.

> You will be careful, if you are wise;
> How you touch Men's Religion, or Credit, or Eyes.

> After Fish,
> Milk do not wish.

> Against Diseases here, the strongest Fence,
> Is the defensive Virtue, Abstinence.

If thou dost ill, the joy fades, not the pains;
If well, the pain doth fade, the joy remains.

To err is human, to repent divine, to persist devilish.

Money & Man a mutual Friendship show:
Man makes *false* Money, Money makes Man so.

Industry pays Debts, Despair encreases them.

Bright as the day and as the morning fair,
Such *Cloe* is, & common as the air.

Here comes *Glib-tongue*: who can out-flatter a Dedication; and lie, like
ten Epitaphs.

Hope and a Red-Rag, are Baits for Men and Mackrel.

With the old Almanack and the old Year,
Leave thy old Vices, tho' ever so dear.

1743

How few there are who have courage enough to own their Faults, or
resolution enough to mend them!

Men differ daily, about things which are subject to Sense, is it likely
then they should agree about things invisible.

Mark with what insolence and pride,

> Blown *Bufo* takes his haughty stride;
> As if no toad was toad beside.

Ill Company is like a dog who dirts those most, that he loves best.

> In prosperous fortunes be modest and wise,
> The greatest may fall, and the lowest may rise:
> But insolent People that fall in disgrace,
> Are wretched and no-body pities their Case.

Sorrow is dry.

The World is full of fools and faint hearts; and yet every one has courage
enough to bear the misfortunes, and wisdom enough to manage the
Affairs of his neighbour.

Beware, beware! He'll cheat 'ithout scruple, who can without fear.

The D—l wipes his B—ch with poor Folks Pride.

> Content and Riches seldom meet together,
> Riches take thou, contentment I had rather.

> Speak with contempt of none, from slave to king,
> The meanest Bee hath, and will use, a sting.

The church the state, and the poor, are 3 daughters which we should
maintain, but not portion off.

> A little well-gotten will do us more good,
> Than lordships and scepters by Rapine and Blood.

Let all Men know thee, but no man know thee thoroughly: Men freely ford
that see the shallows.

> 'Tis easy to frame a good bold resolution;
> but hard is the Task that concerns execution.

> Cold & cunning come from the north:
> But cunning sans wisdom is nothing worth.

> 'Tis vain to repine,
> Tho' a learned Divine
> Will die *this day* at nine.

Ah simple Man! when a boy two precious jewels were given thee, Time, and
good Advice; one thou hast lost, and the other thrown away.

> *Dick* told his spouse, he durst be bold to swear,
> Whate'er she pray'd for, Heav'n would thwart her pray'r:
> Indeed! says *Nell*, 'tis what I'm pleas'd to hear;
> For now I'll pray for your long life, my dear.

The sleeping Fox catches no poultry. Up! up!

If you'd be wealthy, think of saving, more than of getting: The *Indies* have
not made *Spain* rich, because her Outgoes equal her Incomes.

> Came you from Court? for in your Mien,
> A self-important air is seen.

If you'd have it done, Go: If not, send.

Many a long dispute among Divines may be thus abridg'd,
It is so: It is not so. It is so; It is not so.

Experience keeps a dear school, yet Fools will learn in no other.

How many observe Christ's Birth-day! How few, his Precepts! O! 'tis easier
to keep Holidays than Commandments.

1744

He that drinks his Cyder alone, let him catch his Horse alone.

Who is strong? He that can conquer his bad Habits. Who is rich? He that
rejoices in his Portion.

He that has not got a Wife, is not yet a compleat Man.

What you would seem to be, be really.

If you'd lose a troublesome Visitor, lend him Money.

Tart Words make no Friends: a spoonful of honey will catch more flies
than Gallon of Vinegar.

Make haste slowly.

> Dine with little, sup with less:
> Do better still; sleep supperless.

Industry, Perseverance, & Frugality, make Fortune yield.

I'll warrant ye, goes before *Rashness*; *Who'd-a-tho't it?* comes sneaking after.

Prayers and Provender hinder no Journey.

Hear *Reason*, or she'll make you feel her.

Give me yesterday's Bread, this Day's Flesh, and last Year's Cyder.

Sloth (like Rust) consumes faster than Labour wears: the used Key is always bright.

Light Gains heavy Purses.

Keep thou from the Opportunity, and God will keep thee from the Sin.

Where there's no Law, there's no Bread.

As Pride increases, Fortune declines.

Drive thy Business, or it will drive thee.

A full Belly is the Mother of all Evil.

The same man cannot be both Friend and Flatterer.

He who multiplies Riches multiplies Cares.

An old Man in a House is a good Sign.

Those who are fear'd, are hated.

The Things which hurt, instruct.

The Eye of a Master, will do more Work than his Hand.

A soft Tongue may strike hard.

If you'd be belov'd, make yourself amiable.

A true Friend is the best Possession.

Fear God, and your Enemies will fear you.

> *Epitaph on a Scolding Wife by her Husband.*
> Here my poor *Bridget*'s Corps doth lie,
> she is at rest, —and so am I.

1745

Beware of little Expences, a small Leak will sink a great Ship.

Wars bring scars.

A light purse is a heavy Curse.

As often as we do good, we sacrifice.

> Help, Hands;
> For I have no Lands.

It's common for Men to give 6 pretended Reasons instead of one real one.

Vanity backbites more than *Malice.*

He's a Fool that cannot conceal his Wisdom.

Great spenders are bad lenders.

All blood is alike ancient.

You may talk too much on the best of subjects.

A Man without ceremony has need of great merit in its place.

No gains without pains.

Had I revenged wrong, I had not worn my skirts so long.

Graft good Fruit all, or graft not at all.

Idleness is the greatest Prodigality.

Old young and old long.

> Punch-coal, cut-candle, and set brand on end,
> is neither good house wife, nor good house-wife's friend.

> He who buys had need have 100 Eyes,
> but one's enough for him that sells the Stuff.

Many complain of their Memory, few of their Judgment.

One Man may be more cunning than another, but not more cunning than every body else.

To God we owe fear and love; to our neighbours justice and charity; to our selves prudence and sobriety.

Fools make feasts and wise men eat them.

Light-heel'd mothers make leaden-heel'd daughters.

The good or ill hap of a good or ill life,

is the good or ill choice of a good or ill wife.

'Tis easier to prevent bad habits than to break them.

Every Man has Assurance enough to boast of his honesty, few of their Understanding.

Interest which blinds some People, enlightens others.

An ounce of wit that is bought,

Is worth a pound that is taught.

He that resolves to mend hereafter, resolves not to mend now.

1746

When the Well's dry, we know the Worth of Water.

He that whines for Glass without G

Take away L and that's he.

A good Wife & Health,

is a Man's best Wealth.

A quarrelsome Man has no good Neighbours.

Wide will wear,

but Narrow will tear.

Silks and Sattins put out the Kitchen Fire.

Vice knows she's ugly, so puts on her Mask.

It's the easiest Thing in the World for a Man to deceive himself.

> Women & Wine, Game & Deceit,
> Make the Wealth small and the Wants great.

All Mankind are beholden to him that is kind to the Good.

A Plowman on his Legs is higher than a Gentleman on his Knees.

Virtue and Happiness are Mother and Daughter.

The generous Mind least regards money, and yet most feels the Want of it.

For one poor Man there are an hundred indigent.

Dost thou love Life? then do not squander Time; for that's the Stuff Life is made of.

Good Sense is a Thing all need, few have, and none think they want.

What's proper, is becoming: See the Blacksmith with his white Silk Apron!

The Tongue is ever turning to the aching Tooth.

Want of Care does us more Damage than Want of Knowledge.

Take Courage, Mortal; Death can't banish thee out of the Universe.

The Sting of a Reproach, is the Truth of it.

Do me the Favour to deny me at once.

The most exquisite Folly is made of Wisdom spun too fine.

A life of leisure, and a life of laziness, are two things.

Mad Kings and mad Bulls, are not to be held by treaties & packthread.

Changing Countries or Beds, cures neither a bad Manager, nor a Fever.

A true great Man will neither trample on a Worm, nor sneak to an Emperor.

> *Tim* and his Handsaw are good in their Place,
> Tho' not fit for preaching or shaving a face.

Half-Hospitality opens his Doors and shuts up his Countenance.

1747

Strive to be the *greatest* Man in your Country, and you may be disappointed; Strive to be the *best*, and you may succeed: He may well win the race that runs by himself.

> 'Tis a strange Forest that has no rotten Wood in't.
> And a strange Kindred that all are good in't.

None know the unfortunate, and the fortunate do not know themselves.

There's a time to wink as well as to see.

Honest *Tom*! you may trust him with a house-full of untold Milstones.

There is no Man so bad, but he secretly respects the Good.

> When there's more Malice shown than Matter:
> On the Writer falls the satyr.

Courage would fight, but *Discretion* won't let him.

Delicate *Dick*! Whisper'd the Proclamation.

Cornelius ought to be *Tacitus*.

> *Pride* and the *Gout*,
> are seldom cur'd throughout.

We are not so sensible of the greatest Health as of the least Sickness.

A good Example is the best sermon.

A Father's a Treasure; a Brother's a Comfort; a Friend is both.

Despair ruins some, Presumption many.

> A quiet Conscience sleeps in Thunder,
> but Rest and Guilt live far asunder.

He that won't be counsell'd, can't be help'd.

Craft must be at charge for clothes, but *Truth* can go naked.

Write Injuries in Dust, Benefits in Marble.

What is Serving God? 'Tis doing Good to Man.

What maintains one Vice would bring up two Children.

Many have been ruin'd by buying good pennyworths.

Better is a little with content than much with contention.

> A Slip of the Foot you may soon recover:
> But a Slip of the Tongue you may never get over.

What signifies your Patience, if you can't find it when you want it.

d. wise, l. foolish.

Time enough, always proves *little enough*.

It is wise not to seek a Secret, and Honest not to reveal it.

A Mob's a Monster; Heads enough, but no Brains.

The Devil sweetens Poison with Honey.

He that cannot bear with other People's Passions, cannot govern his own.

> He that by the Plow would thrive,
> himself must either hold or drive.

1748

> Robbers must exalted be,
> Small ones on the Gallow-Tree,

While greater ones ascend to Thrones,
But what is that to thee or me?

Lost Time is never found again.

To lead a virtuous Life, my Friends, and get to Heaven in Season,
You've just so much more Need of *Faith*, as you have less
of *Reason*.

To avoid Pleurisies, *&c.* in cool Weather; Fevers, Fluxes,
&c. in hot; beware of *Over-Eating* and *Over-Heating*.

The Heathens when they dy'd, went to Bed without a Candle.

Knaves & Nettles are akin;
stroak 'em kindly, yet they'll sting.

Life with Fools consists in Drinking;
With the wise Man Living's Thinking.

Sell-cheap kept Shop on *Goodwin Sands*, and yet had Store of Custom.

Liberality is not giving much but giving wisely.

Suspicion may be no Fault, but shewing it may be a great one.

He that's secure is not safe.

The second Vice is Lying; the first is Running in Debt.

The Muses love the Morning.

> Two Faults of one a Fool will make;
> He half repairs, that owns & does forsake.

> *Harry Smatter,*
> has a Mouth for every Matter.

When you're good to others, you are best to yourself.

Half Wits talk much but say little.

If *Jack's* in love, he's no judge of *Jill's* Beauty.

Most Fools think they are only ignorant.

Pardoning the Bad, is injuring the Good.

He is not well-bred, that cannot bear Ill-Breeding in others.

> In Christmas feasting pray take care;
> Let not your table be a Snare;
> but with the Poor God's Bounty share.

1749

Wealth and Content are not always Bed-fellows.

Wise Men learn by others harms; Fools by their own.

The end of Passion is the beginning of Repentance.

Words may shew a man's Wit, but *Actions* his Meaning.

'Tis a well spent penny that saves a groat.

Many Foxes grow grey, but few grow good.

Presumption first blinds a Man, then sets him a running.

> A cold April,
> The Barn will fill.

Content makes poor men rich; Discontent makes rich Men poor.

Too much plenty makes Mouth dainty.

If *Passion* drives, let *Reason* hold the Reins.

> Neither trust, nor contend, nor lay wagers, nor lend;
> And you'll have peace to your Lives end.

Drink does not drown *Care*, but waters it, and makes it grow faster.

Who dainties love, shall Beggars prove.

A Man has no more *Goods* than he gets Good by.

Welcome, Mischief, if thou comest alone.

Different Sects like different clocks, may be all near the matter,
'tho they don't quite agree.

If your head is wax, don't walk in the Sun.

Pretty & *Witty*,
 will wound if they hit ye.

Having been poor is no shame, but being ashamed of it, is.

'Tis a laudable Ambition, that aims at being better than his Neighbours.

The wise Man draws more Advantage from his Enemies, than the Fool
 from his Friends.

All would live long, but none would be old.

Declaiming against Pride, is not always a Sign of Humility.

Neglect kills Injuries, Revenge increases them.

9 Men in 10 are suicides.

Doing an Injury puts you below your Enemy; *Revenging* one makes
 you but *even* with him; *Forgiving* it sets you *above* him.

Most of the Learning in use, is of no great Use.

Great Good-nature, without Prudence, is a great Misfortune.

> Keep Conscience clear,
> Then never fear.

A Man in a Passion rides a mad Horse.

> Reader farewel, all Happiness attend thee;
> May each New-Year, better and richer find thee.

There are three Things extreamly hard, Steel, a Diamond and to know one's self.

Hunger is the best Pickle.

He is a Governor that governs his Passions, and he a Servant that serves them.

A Cypher and Humility make the other Figures & Virtues of ten-fold Value.

If it were not for the Belly, the Back might wear Gold.

Wouldst thou confound thine Enemy, be good thy self.

Pride is as loud a Beggar as *Want*, and a great deal more saucy.

Pay what you owe, and what you're worth you'll know.

Sorrow is good for nothing but Sin.

Many a Man thinks he is buying Pleasure, when he is really selling himself a Slave to it.

Tis hard (but glorious) to be poor and honest: An empty Sack can hardly stand upright; but if it does, 'tis a stout one!

He that can bear a Reproof, and mend by it, if he is not wise, is in a fair way of being so.

Sound, & sound Doctrine, may pass through a Ram's Horn, and a Preacher, without straitening the one, or amending the other.

Clean your Finger, before you point at my Spots.

He that spills the Rum, loses that only; He that drinks it, often loses both that and himself.

> That Ignorance makes devout, if right the Notion,
> 'Troth, *Rufus*, thou'rt a Man of great Devotion.

Those that have much Business must have much Pardon.

Discontented Minds, and Fevers of the Body are not to be cured by changing Beds or Businesses.

> Little Strokes,
> Fell great Oaks.

You may be too cunning for One, but not for All.

Genius without Education is like Silver in the Mine.

Many would live by their Wits, but break for want of Stock.

Poor *Plain dealing*! dead without Issue!

You can bear your own Faults, and why not a Fault in your Wife.

Tho' Modesty is a Virtue, Bashfulness is a Vice.

> Hide not your Talents, they for Use were made.
> What's a Sun-Dial in the Shade!

What signifies knowing the Names, if you know not the Natures of Things.

Tim was so learned, that he could name a Horse in nine Languages;
So ignorant, that he bought a Cow to ride on.

The Golden Age never was the present Age.

'Tis a Shame that your Family is an Honour to you! You ought to be an Honour to your Family.

Glass, China, and Reputation, are easily crack'd, and never well mended.

1751

Pray don't burn my House to roast your Eggs.

Some *Worth* it argues, a Friend's *Worth* to know;
Virtue to own the Virtue of a Foe.

Prosperity discovers Vice, Adversity Virtue.

Many a Man would have been worse, if his Estate had been better.

He that is conscious of a Stink in his Breeches, is jealous of every Wrinkle in another's Nose.

Love and *Tooth-ach* have many Cures, but none infallible, except *Possession* and *Dispossession*.

Most People return small Favours, acknowledge middling ones, and repay great ones with Ingratitude.

We may give Advice, but we cannot give Conduct.

> Fond Pride of Dress is sure an empty Curse;
> E're *Fancy* you consult, consult your Purse.

Youth is pert and positive, *Age* modest and doubting: So Ears of Corn when young and light, stand bolt upright, but hang their Heads when weighty, full, and ripe.

'Tis easier to suppress the first Desire, than to satisfy all that follow it.

Don't judge of Mens Wealth or Piety, by their *Sunday* Appearances.

Friendship increases by visiting Friends, but by visiting seldom.

If your Riches are yours, why don't you take them with you to the t'other World?

What more valuable than Gold? Diamonds. Than Diamonds? Virtue.

To-day is Yesterday's Pupil.

If worldly Goods cannot save me from Death, they ought not to hinder me of eternal Life.

'Tis great Confidence in a Friend to tell him *your* Faults, greater to tell him *his*.

Talking against Religion is unchaining a Tyger; The Beast let loose may worry his Deliverer.

Ambition often spends foolishly what *Avarice* had wickedly collected.

Pillgarlic was in the *Accusative* Case, and bespoke a Lawyer in the *Vocative*, who could not understand him till he made use of the *Dative*.

> Great Estates may venture more;
> Little Boats must keep near Shore.

Nice Eaters seldom meet with a good Dinner.

Not to oversee Workmen, is to leave them your Purse open.

The Wise and Brave dares own that he was wrong.

Cunning proceeds from Want of Capacity.

The Proud hate Pride—in others.

Who judges best of a Man, his Enemies or himself?

Drunkenness, that worst of Evils, makes some Men Fools, some Beasts, some Devils.

'Tis not a Holiday that's not kept holy.

1752

Observe old *Vellum*; he praises former Times, as if he'd a mind to sell 'em.

Kings have long Arms, but Misfortune longer: Let none think themselves out of her Reach.

The busy Man has few idle Visitors; to the boiling Pot the Flies come not.

For want of a Nail the Shoe is lost; for want of a Shoe, the Horse is lost; for want of a Horse the Rider is lost.

Calamity and Prosperity are the Touchstones of Integrity.

The Prodigal generally does more Injustice than the Covetous.

Generous Minds are all of kin.

'Tis more noble to forgive, and more manly to despise, than to revenge an Injury.

A Brother may not be a Friend, but a Friend will always be a Brother.

Meanness is the Parent of Insolence.

Mankind are very odd Creatures: One Half censure what they practise, the other half practise what they censure; the rest always say and do as they ought.

Severity is often Clemency; Clemency Severity.

Bis dat qui cito dat: He gives twice that gives soon; *i.e.* he will soon be called upon to give again.

A Temper to bear much, will have much to bear.

Pride dines upon Vanity, sups on Contempt.

Great Merit is coy, as well as great Pride.

An undutiful Daughter, will prove an unmanageable Wife.

Old Boys have their Playthings as well as young Ones; the Difference is only in the Price.

The too obliging Temper is evermore disobliging itself.

Hold your Council before Dinner; the full Belly hates Thinking as well as Acting.

The Brave and the Wise can both pity and excuse; when Cowards and Fools shew no Mercy.

Ceremony is not Civility; nor Civility Ceremony.

If Man could have Half his Wishes, he would double his Troubles.

It is ill Jesting with the Joiner's Tools, worse with the Doctor's.

Children and Princes will quarrel for Trifles.

Praise to the undeserving, is severe Satyr.

Success has ruin'd many a Man.

> Great Pride and Meanness sure are near ally'd;
> Or thin Partitions do their Bounds divide.

1753

'Tis against some Mens Principle to pay Interest, and seems against others Interest to pay the Principal.

Philosophy as well as Foppery often changes Fashion.

Setting too good an Example is a Kind of Slander seldom forgiven;
    'tis *Scandalum Magnatum*.

A great Talker may be no Fool, but he is one that relies on him.

When Reason preaches, if you won't hear her she'll box your Ears.

It is not Leisure that is not used.

The Good-will of the Governed will be starv'd, if not fed by the good
    Deeds of the Governors.

Paintings and Fightings are best seen at a distance.

> If you would reap Praise you must sow the Seeds,
> Gentle Words and useful Deeds.

Ignorance leads Men into a Party, and *Shame* keeps them from getting
    out again.

Haste makes Waste.

Many have quarrel'd about Religion, that never practis'd it.

Sudden Power is apt to be insolent, *Sudden Liberty* saucy;
    that behaves best which has grown gradually.

He that best understands the World, least likes it.

> *Anger* is never without a Reason, but seldom with a good One.

He that is of Opinion Money will do every Thing, may well be suspected of doing every Thing for Money.

An ill Wound, but not an ill Name, may be healed.

When out of Favour, none know thee; when in, thou dost not know thyself.

A lean Award is better than a fat Judgment.

God, *Parents*, and *Instructors*, can never be requited.

He that builds before he counts the Cost, acts foolishly; and he that counts before he builds, finds he did not count wisely.

Patience in Market, is worth Pounds in a Year.

Danger is Sauce for Prayers.

If you have no Honey in your Pot, have some in your Mouth.

A Pair of good Ears will drain dry an hundred Tongues.

Serving God is Doing Good to Man, but Praying is thought an easier Service, and therefore more generally chosen.

Nothing humbler than *Ambition*, when it is about to climb.

The discontented Man finds no easy Chair.

Virtue and a Trade, are a Child's best Portion.

Gifts much expected, are *paid*, not *given*.

The first Degree of Folly, is to conceit one's self wise; the second to profess it; the third to despise Counsel.

Take heed of the Vinegar of sweet Wine, and the Anger of Good-nature.

The Bell calls others to Church, but itself never minds the Sermon.

Cut the Wings of your Hens and Hopes, lest they lead you a weary Dance after them.

In Rivers & bad Governments, the lightest Things swim at top.

The Cat in Gloves catches no Mice.

If you'd know the Value of Money, go and borrow some.

The Horse thinks one thing, and he that saddles him another.

Love your Neighbour; yet don't pull down your Hedge.

When *Prosperity* was well mounted, she let go the Bridle, and soon came tumbling out of the Saddle.

Some make Conscience of wearing a Hat in the Church, who make none of robbing the Altar.

In the Affairs of this World Men are saved, not by Faith, but by the Want of it.

Friendship cannot live with *Ceremony*, nor without *Civility*.

Praise little, dispraise less.

The learned Fool writes his Nonsense in better Language than the unlearned; but still 'tis Nonsense.

A Child thinks 20 *Shillings* and 20 Years can scarce ever be spent.

Don't think so much of your own Cunning, as to forget other Mens: A cunning Man is overmatch'd by a cunning Man and a Half.

Willows are weak, but they bind the Faggot.

You may give a Man an Office, but you cannot give him Discretion.

He that doth what he should not, shall feel what he would not.

To be intimate with a foolish Friend, is like going to bed to a Razor.

Little Rogues easily become great Ones.

You may sometimes be much in the wrong, in owning your being in the right.

Friends are the true Sceptres of Princes.

Where Sense is wanting, every thing is wanting.

Many Princes sin with *David*, but few repent with him.

He that hath no *ill* Fortune will be troubled with *good*.

> For Age and Want save while you may;
> No Morning Sun lasts a whole Day.

Learning to the Studious; Riches to the Careful; Power to the Bold; Heaven to the Virtuous.

Now glad the Poor with *Christmas* Cheer;
Thank God you're able so to end the Year.

1755

A Man without a Wife, is but half a Man.

Speak little, do much.

He that would travel much, should eat little.

When the Wine enters, out goes the Truth.

If you would be loved, love and be loveable.

Ask and have, is sometimes dear buying.

The hasty Bitch brings forth blind Puppies.

Where there is Hunger, Law is not regarded; and where Law is not regarded, there will be Hunger.

Two dry Sticks will burn a green One.

The honest Man takes Pains, and then enjoys Pleasures; the Knave takes Pleasure, and then suffers Pains.

Think of three Things, whence you came, where you are going, and to whom you must account.

Necessity has no Law; Why? Because 'tis not to be had without Money.

There was never a good Knife made of bad Steel.

The Wolf sheds his Coat once a Year, his Disposition never.

> *Who is wise?* He that learns from every One.
> *Who is powerful?* He that governs his Passions.
> *Who is rich?* He that is content.
> *Who is that?* Nobody.

A full Belly brings forth every Evil.

The Day is short, the Work great, the Workmen lazy, the Wages high, the Master urgeth; Up, then, and be doing.

The Doors of Wisdom are never shut.

Much Virtue in Herbs, little in Men.

The Master's Eye will do more Work than both his Hands.

When you taste Honey, remember Gall.

Being ignorant is not so much a Shame, as being unwilling to learn.

God gives all Things to Industry.

An hundred Thieves cannot strip one naked Man, especially if his Skin's off.

Diligence overcomes Difficulties, Sloth makes them.

Neglect mending a small Fault, and 'twill soon be a great One.

Bad Gains are truly Losses.

A long Life may not be good enough, but a good Life is long enough.

Be at War with your Vices, at Peace with your Neighbours, and let every New-Year find you a better Man.

1756

A Change of *Fortune* hurts a wise Man no more than a Change of the *Moon*.

> Does Mischief, Misconduct, & Warrings displease ye;
> Think there's a Providence, 'twill make ye easy.

Mine is better than *Ours*.

Love your Enemies, for they tell you your Faults.

He that has a Trade, has an Office of Profit and Honour.

Be civil to *all*; serviceable to *many*; familiar with *few*; Friend to *one*; Enemy to *none*.

Vain-Glory flowereth, but beareth no Fruit.

Laws *too gentle* are seldom *obeyed*; *too severe*, seldom *executed*.

Trouble springs from *Idleness*; *Toil* from *Ease*.

Love, and be *loved*.

A wise Man will desire no more, than what he may get justly, use soberly, distribute chearfully, and leave contentedly.

The diligent Spinner has a large Shift.

A false Friend and a Shadow, attend only while the Sun shines.

To-morrow, every Fault is to be amended; but that *To-morrow* never comes.

> Plough deep, while Sluggards sleep;
> And you shall have Corn, to sell and to keep.

Sampson with his *strong Body*, had a *weak Head*, or he would not have laid it in a Harlot's Lap.

> When a Friend deals with a Friend
> Let the Bargain be clear and well penn'd,
> That they may continue Friends to the End.

He that never eats too much, will never be lazy.

To be *proud* of *Knowledge*, is to be *blind* with *Light*; to be *proud* of *Virtue*, is to *poison* yourself with the *Antidote*.

> Get what you can, and what you get, hold;
> 'Tis the *Stone* that will turn all your Lead into Gold.

An honest Man will receive neither *Money* nor *Praise*, that is not his Due.

Saying and *Doing*, have quarrel'd and parted.

Tell me my Faults, and mend your own.

He that would rise at Court, must begin by Creeping.

Many a Man's own Tongue gives Evidence against his Understanding.

Nothing dries sooner than a Tear.

'Tis easier to build two Chimneys, than maintain one in Fuel.

Anger warms the Invention, but overheats the Oven.

It is Ill-Manners to silence a Fool, and Cruelty to let him go on.

Scarlet, Silk and Velvet, have put out the Kitchen Fire.

He that would catch Fish, must venture his Bait.

Men take more pains to mask than mend.

One *To-day* is worth two *To-morrows*.

The way to be safe, is never to be secure.

Dally not with other Folks Women or Money.

Work as if you were to live 100 Years, Pray as if you were to die To-morrow.

Pride breakfasted with *Plenty*, dined with *Poverty*, supped with *Infamy*.

Retirement does not always secure Virtue; *Lot* was upright in the City, wicked in the Mountain.

Idleness is the Dead Sea, that swallows all Virtues: Be active in Business, that *Temptation* may miss her Aim: The Bird that sits, is easily shot.

Shame and the *Dry-belly-ach* were Diseases of the last Age; this seems to be cured of them.

Tho' the Mastiff be gentle, yet bite him not by the Lip.

Great-Alms-giving, lessens no Man's Living.

The royal Crown cures not the Head-ach.

Act uprightly, and despise Calumny; Dirt may stick to a Mud Wall, but not to polish'd Marble.

The *Borrower* is a Slave to the *Lender*; the *Security* to *both*.

Singularity in the right, hath ruined many: Happy those who are convinced of the general Opinion.

Proportion your Charity to the Strength of your Estate, or God will proportion your Estate to the Weakness of your Charity.

The Tongue offends, and the Ears get the Cuffing.

Sleep without Supping, and you'll rise without owing for it.

> When other Sins grow old by Time,
> Then Avarice is in its prime,
> Yet feed the Poor at *Christmas* time.

1758

One *Nestor* is worth two *Ajaxes*.

> When you're an Anvil, hold you still;
> When you're a Hammer, strike your Fill.

When Knaves betray each other, one can scarce be blamed, or the other pitied.

He that carries a small Crime easily, will carry it on when it comes to be an Ox.

Happy *Tom Crump*, ne'er sees his own Hump.

Fools need Advice most, but wise Men only are the better for it.

Silence is not always a Sign of Wisdom, but Babbling is ever a Mark of Folly.

Great Modesty often hides great Merit.

You may delay, but *Time* will not.

Virtue may not always make a Face handsome, but *Vice* will certainly make it ugly.

Prodigality of *Time*, produces Poverty of Mind as well as of Estate.

Content is the Philosopher's Stone, that turns all it touches into Gold.

He that's content, hath enough; He that complains, has too much.

Pride gets into the Coach, and *Shame* mounts behind.

The first Mistake in publick Business, is the going into it.

Half the Truth is often a great Lie.

The Way to see by *Faith*, is to shut the Eye of *Reason*: The Morning Daylight appears plainer when you put out your Candle.

A full Belly makes a dull Brain: The Muses starve in a Cook's Shop.

Spare and have is better than *spend and crave*.

Good-Will, like the Wind, floweth where it listeth.

The Honey is sweet, but the Bee has a Sting.

In a corrupt Age, the putting the World in order would breed Confusion; then e'en mind your own Business.

To serve the Publick faithfully, and at the same time please it entirely, is impracticable.

Proud Modern Learning despises the antient: *School-men* are now laught at by *School-boys*.

Men often *mistake* themselves, seldom *forget* themselves.

The idle Man is the Devil's Hireling; whose Livery is Rags, whose Diet and Wages are Famine and Diseases.

Rob not God, nor the Poor, lest thou ruin thyself; the Eagle snatcht a Coal from the Altar, but it fired her Nest.

> With bounteous Cheer,
> Conclude the Year.